BABY SIGN LANGUAGE SONGS AND GAMES

BABY SIGN LANGUAGE

Songs & Games

AGES
0-3

Lane Rebelo

ROCKRIDGE
PRESS

65 Fun Activities for Easy Everyday Learning

Interior and Cover Designer: Amanda Kirk
Art Producer: Janice Ackerman
Editor: Mo Mozuch
Production Manager: Riley Hoffman
Production Editor: Ashley Polikoff

Illustration: © 2019 Boris Stoilov
Illustration, pp. x-xiii: © 2019 Natalia Sanabria
Cover Photography: © Peopleimages/iStock
Author Photo Courtesy of Jacquelyn Warner

Paperback ISBN: 978-1-63878-494-4
eBook ISBN: 978-1-63878-537-8
R0

For Courtney Arseneault and Jessica Wentworth,
whose passion for early childhood inspired me and made
the early years magical for our family.

Contents

Introduction

WELCOME TO *BABY SIGN LANGUAGE SONGS AND GAMES*! I'm so excited you picked up this book. I believe it holds the key to unlocking endless fun and bonding with your baby or toddler.

Teaching new parents and early childhood professionals how to have fun and succeed with baby signing is my passion. Through my Tiny Signs® program and my popular baby sign language books, I've helped tens of thousands of parents and caregivers succeed in using basic American Sign Language (ASL) vocabulary to communicate with their preverbal babies and toddlers. *Baby Sign Language Songs and Games* is my fourth baby sign language book, and I am so excited to share it with you!

One of my favorite parts of writing my first two books, *Baby Sign Language Made Easy* and *The Complete Guide to Baby Sign Language*, was coming up with simple songs and activities at the end of each chapter to help families incorporate signing into their days. When I taught in-person classes in the Boston area, I always enjoyed seeing the children engage with movement and song. Many of you have shared with me how much fun you've had using those ideas to play and practice signing. Now I get to share a whole book's worth of songs and games for you and your little one to enjoy!

It's easy to look up a sign online to learn how to do it. (In fact, with your book purchase, you can access a video dictionary of all the signs in this book at TinySigns.com/book-owner.) Still, many parents struggle to figure out how to teach the signs to their babies. This book will provide you with 65 fun and easy ways to sing and play with your baby while also teaching them useful ASL vocabulary. Before you know it, both you and your little one will have expanded your signing vocabulary all through simply enjoying time together.

The songs and activities in this book are meant to be fun, not stressful. If you don't have the supplies for one of the games, just improvise or move on to the next one. As you go through the book, you'll find that you and your baby will enjoy some activities more than others, and that's just fine! Repeat the ones your baby loves over and over.

Please don't forget: All babies are different and will learn at their own pace and have their own preferences. Follow your own instincts and pay attention to your baby's reactions to each of the songs and games. Let their responses be your cue for what to do more of and what to skip. There's no right way to use these activities, so, again, just have fun!

How to Use This Book

THIS BOOK IS WRITTEN FOR parents and caregivers of infants and toddlers looking for fun and easy ways to incorporate sign language and language-building activities into their day. Throughout the book, you'll notice that key vocabulary words are written in caps to highlight them in the text. Words you see in bold caps are intended to be both signed and spoken. For example, in the phrase "Twinkle, twinkle, little **STAR**," the word *star* should be signed and spoken simultaneously.

This book is divided into two parts. Part 1 provides a brief overview of baby sign language, including what to expect and answers to common questions. In part 2, you'll find all the songs and games you're looking for! The activities are broken up into three chapters, grouping the songs and games by vocabulary themes, including Baby's Busy Day, Baby's Favorite Things, and Baby's Big World.

In each of these chapters, you'll find a mix of songs and games you can use to practice signs and build language skills. Most of the songs will be ones you already know and love, while others might be new songs set to familiar tunes. Remember to always supervise closely when using items that aren't intended for babies, and never leave your baby alone with objects not meant for children under three.

Each of the songs and games in this book will help increase your comfort and confidence in using signs. You and your baby are going to have so much fun singing, playing, and *signing* together!

ASL Alphabet and Numbers 1-10

 Make a fist with palm facing out and thumb pointing up at the side.

A

 Make a flat hand with palm facing out, fingers touching, and thumb tucked in.

B

 Curve your hand into a *C* shape.

C

 Curve all fingers to touch thumb except pointer, which is extended up.

D

 Let all fingertips rest along thumb with palm facing out.

E

 Bend pointer finger to touch thumb with fingers open, palm facing out.

F

 Close hand in a fist with pointer finger and thumb pointing to the side, palm facing in.

G

 Close hand in a fist with pointer and middle fingers pointing to the side, palm facing in.

H

 Close hand with pinky finger pointing up and palm facing out.

I

 Draw a *J* in the air with pinky finger.

J

 Raise pointer and middle fingers up in a *V* shape with thumb tucked into the base of the *V*.

K

 Raise pointer finger up and thumb to the side to make an *L* shape with palm facing out.

L

M With palm facing out, fold first three fingers over thumb, which is holding down pinky.

N Place first two fingers over thumb, which is holding down pinky and ring finger, with palm facing out.

O Touch all fingers to thumb to make an *O* shape.

P Point pointer and middle fingers down in a *V* shape with thumb tucked into the base of the *V*.

Q Close hand in a fist with pointer finger and thumb pointing down.

R Twist pointer and middle fingers together with palm facing out.

S Close hand in a fist with thumb over closed fingers and palm facing out.

T Close hand with thumb tucked between first two fingers and palm facing out.

U Point pointer and middle fingers up, touching, with palm facing out.

V Point pointer and middle fingers up and spread into a *V* shape with palm facing out.

W Point first three fingers up and spread into a *W* shape with palm facing out.

X Close hand in a fist with pointer finger up and bent, palm facing out.

Y Close hand with thumb and pinky extended, palm facing out.

Z Draw a *Z* in the air with pointer finger.

Close hand with pointer finger pointing up and palm facing either in or out.

1

 Point pointer and middle fingers up and spread into a *V* shape with palm facing either in or out.

2

 Spread pointer finger, middle finger, and thumb open and extended with palm facing either in or out.

3

 Point all fingers up and spread open with thumb tucked in, palm facing either in or out.

4

 Open hand wide with palm facing either in or out.

5

 Touch pinky finger to thumb, with remaining fingers spread open and palm facing out.

6

 Touch ring finger to thumb, with remaining fingers spread open and palm facing out.

7

 Touch middle finger to thumb, with remaining fingers spread open and palm facing out.

8

 Touch pointer finger to thumb, with remaining fingers spread open and palm facing out.

9

 Make a thumbs-up gesture with one hand and give it a little shake.

10

PART 1

Before You Get Started

Before we dive into the songs and games, let's take a minute to review what baby sign language is and how it can help support your baby's overall language development.

In this section, you'll get an overview of baby sign language and what to expect in the weeks and months ahead. We'll go over how signing works in tandem with your baby's budding speech and language skills. We'll also review realistic expectations based on your baby's age. In this section you'll also find answers to the common questions parents often ask me.

If you've recently read either of my books *Baby Sign Language Made Easy* or *The Complete Guide to Baby Sign Language*, you can skip this section and jump straight to part 2, where you'll find the songs and games. However, if it's been a while since you read either of those titles, the rest of part 1 will help you brush up on the basics and get ready to go!

CHAPTER 1

What Is Baby Sign Language?

Baby sign language is a *communication technique,* not an actual language. Baby signing blends both spoken language and sign language to give babies the tools to communicate while their speech is still developing.

American Sign Language (ASL) is the rich and complex language of the Deaf community in the United States and Canada. For the purposes of early communication with hearing babies, we'll be using individual ASL signs paired with spoken language. This hybrid of spoken English and ASL vocabulary is what I mean when I say "baby sign language." Baby sign language can be a combination of any spoken language (English, Spanish, Mandarin, Urdu, etc.) and sign language (ASL, British Sign Language, Auslan, etc.).

You can also use signs with more than one spoken language if you are a bilingual family. One of my bilingual students described signing as a "zipper" that connects the two spoken languages in their home, and I just loved that analogy. Signing is a wonderfully visual way to help your baby connect the meaning of a word in two (or more!) spoken languages.

There are many benefits to supplementing early communication with sign language, including improved communication and language skills, reduced frustration for babies and caregivers, improved bonding and connection, and more. This book will help you realize all of these benefits, including my personal favorite: signing is just plain fun!

SIGNING AT EVERY AGE AND STAGE

Signing with your 5-month-old is an entirely different experience from signing with your 15-month-old. Babies develop and change rapidly, acquiring skills today that they didn't have yesterday. It's important to take this into consideration when using baby sign language!

Keep in mind as you read through the following sections that all babies are unique and advance at their own pace. These are general guidelines covering large periods of development. While a 7-month-old and an 11-month-old are very different, they would still fall within the 6-to-12-month range for these overarching guidelines. And if you have any concerns or questions about your little one's speech and language development, make sure to talk with your pediatrician at their next checkup.

Here's some advice every parent needs to hear periodically, and it applies to baby signing: Do your best not to get caught up in comparing your little one with other babies or thinking too much about milestones. The most important thing is to enjoy it!

0 to 6 Months

During the first 6 months, your baby recognizes and loves hearing your voice. Talking and singing is a great way to soothe them while also supporting language development. You'll find lots of songs to sing and sign to your baby in part 2 of this book.

Your baby's vision is still developing during this time, so be sure any signing you do is close enough so they can see your hands and face. By around 4 to 6 months, your little one will start moving their eyes in the direction of sounds. As you speak and sign, your baby might follow the sound of your voice to look at your face. When possible, move your hands closer to your face when you sign so your baby sees it.

During this time, your baby will begin smiling and cooing in response to your voice. **You might also notice your baby responding to your use of sign language.** For example, your little one might widen their eyes and kick their legs in response to you saying and signing **MILK**. **Some babies *might* start signing toward the end of this age range, although it's more common for babies to start signing in the 8-to-12-month range.** If you begin using baby sign language in this stage, it's very important to be patient and not get discouraged!

6 to 12 Months

As your baby learns to move into a sitting position, a whole new world of learning and exploring opens up! Once your baby can sit independently, they'll be able to use their hands to reach, grab, and—yes—sign!

It is during the latter part of the 6-to-12-month period that we often see babies start using signs. But before that first sign ever emerges, you'll notice your baby communicating by reaching, grabbing, and even pointing (with an open hand).

As babies in this stage begin to explore their world, they begin to show preferences for certain items and activities. **Signing is so helpful to support your baby's communication. Choosing signs based on your little one's favorite foods, toys, and games will make things easier for everyone!**

Your little one's vocalizations will become more complex during this time, moving from grunts, coos, and even screeches to babbling that sounds more like words ("da da da da da"). Around the time of your baby's first birthday, you may even hear their first spoken word!

If your baby is 12 months old and hasn't started signing yet, not to worry. Stick with it and you'll see that first sign very soon!

12+ Months

By your baby's first birthday, their receptive language (what your baby understands) has really exploded, while their expressive language (what your baby can communicate) is often quite limited. Baby sign language is the perfect solution to bridge this gap as young toddlers understand many words but are not able to say them just yet.

Signing with toddlers is great fun, as they tend to pick up signing quickly (within a few days to a few weeks) and their overall language development is exploding. From 12 to 24 months, your toddler will go from saying their first word to saying dozens of words and even combining them into simple sentences.

This is also the time when your baby will go from taking their first steps to running! There is so much fun to be had as your toddler becomes more mobile and interactive. **Signing is a wonderful tool for busy babies during this stage, as it keeps both their minds and bodies active and learning!** Your baby will love learning signs for their favorite foods, toys, animals, and activities.

Your baby can learn dozens of signs and might even use them along with spoken words as speech develops. Signs can help clarify toddlers' early words, which can be notoriously difficult to understand.

•••• MAKING SIGNING FUN! ••••

Ask any of my students from the decade-plus that I've been teaching baby sign language, and they'll tell you that I always say the two biggest secrets to baby signing success are (1) working with your baby's interests and (2) making signing *fun*! Useful signs (like **MILK, EAT,** and **BED**) are helpful for getting baby's needs met and reducing frustration, but playful signs (like **DOG, BALL,** and **LIGHT**) are often of greater interest and therefore more motivating for little ones.

Songs and nursery rhymes are one of my favorite ways to introduce signs to little ones, because babies love music and love listening to their favorite people (that's you!) sing to them. Songs and nursery rhymes tend to be repetitive, providing lots of opportunities to highlight key words and demonstrate signs. By adding signs to the songs you are likely already singing to your baby (like "The Itsy Bitsy Spider," page 95), you'll make the process of learning a useful sign, like **WATER** ("went up the **WATER** spout"), more engaging and motivating for your little one.

Being silly and playing are also key to your baby sign language success. If that's not something that comes naturally to you, that's okay. The games and activities in this book will give you all kinds of ideas for unlocking your playful side and having a blast with your baby!

THE LEARNING PROCESS

There are a few stages of learning between showing your baby a sign for the first time and your baby signing back to you on their own. First, your baby watches your hands and face as you speak and sign. Next, they will show that they understand your sign by reacting appropriately. (For example, they might look around for the cat when you say and sign **CAT**.) Soon they might start "babbling" with their hands, mimicking your signing by doing the same motion over and over (like signing **MILK** repeatedly when they've just had some and are full). Then, finally, the moment you've been waiting for comes: Your baby signs on their own to communicate with you. Hooray!

The following point is very important to remember: Even once your baby starts signing intentionally to communicate, their signs will likely *not* look like yours. Just like early words, early signs are usually rough approximations of the actual signs. Just as your baby might say "muh muh" before they clearly say "mommy," they might clap their hands or knock both fists together instead of signing **MORE** with perfectly formed ASL hand shapes. This is totally fine and nothing to worry about! In fact, you should expect this. Respond to your baby's sign approximation as if they nailed it perfectly, and continue to model the correct sign. With time, as your little one's motor skills evolve, their signs will get more precise. You might even find you miss those adorable "mistakes" they made when they first started signing. As a mom of "big kids," I know I do!

CHAPTER 2

Answers to Commonly Asked Questions

You might have questions about how to get started with signing: When do I start? How many signs should I use? You might know some basics but have bigger questions: How will baby sign language affect my baby's speech development? How can I get other family members and caregivers on board? Or you might have questions that get into some of the details of signing with baby: Does it matter which hand I use? How do I get my little one to do the signs correctly? In the next few pages, I'll answer these questions and many more so you can enjoy the activities in this book with confidence.

FREQUENTLY ASKED QUESTIONS

Let me begin by putting your mind at ease about the big-picture questions, like how signing will affect your baby's speech development. This is one of the most common questions I've gotten in the many years I've been teaching baby sign language. You may have some well-meaning but uninformed friends or relatives who worry that this "signing stuff" will slow down or discourage your baby from talking. You can assure them that the research shows baby sign language has a positive impact on speech and language development. It is evidence based, and if you want to surprise the naysayers, tell them that babies who use sign language tend to speak earlier and have larger vocabularies!

I want to cover some of the many other questions I've been asked frequently over the years. You might have them, too. I've pulled together a list of the top eight questions parents and caregivers ask, and I hope they fill in the gaps for you.

Is it too early or too late to start using sign language with my baby?

Whether your baby is 4 months old, 14 months old, or even 24 months old, it's never too early or too late to start signing!

The primary benefit of baby signing is to bridge the communication gap that exists before little ones begin to talk. We know that speech development doesn't happen overnight! Instead, there are many little steps between baby's first word (typically around 12 months old) and putting words together into simple sentences (usually around two years old). Signing is the perfect tool to organically build communication while your little one's speech develops.

Remember, all babies are different, and milestones provide a rough guideline of what to expect. *Most* babies start signing in the 8-to-12-month range. Still, some babies will begin earlier, and some will begin later. Here's the key takeaway for you, the parent or caregiver: It's so important to have realistic expectations when you're first getting started with signing, because the younger your baby is, the more patient you'll need to be. Be patient, stick with it, and don't get discouraged.

For preverbal babies, sign language is incredibly useful. But it's also a lifesaver for both toddlers and parents as you start to decode those hard-to-understand early words. For example, if your little one says "buh-buh," you might think they're saying "bye-bye" or asking for their stuffed bear. But if they say "buh-buh" while also signing **BALL**, you'll know *exactly* what they're saying. Baby will be delighted when you give them a ball, and you'll be delighted because you'll think, "Wow! I knew what they wanted." You can be certain baby will try that again soon.

Is baby sign language the same thing as ASL?

The signs you'll learn in this book are American Sign Language (ASL) vocabulary; however, signing a single word here and there while speaking is not the same as using ASL. What is commonly referred to as "baby signing" or "baby sign language" is a communication technique, not an actual language.

Baby signing is sign language vocabulary (a collection of individual signs) that is paired with one (or more) spoken languages. It's a common misconception that there is just one "sign language." The truth is, there is a beautiful tapestry of hundreds of sign languages throughout the world. In this book, all the signs are ASL signs, not made-up gestures for babies. You may even find that these signs don't match those found in other books, which may be using regional variations of ASL signs or invented motions.

When using baby sign language (individual ASL signs paired with speech), what we're focusing on is a communication technique to clarify and support spoken language development for hearing babies and toddlers. This is distinct from full ASL, which is essential for deaf babies' development.

Will sign language confuse my baby? We're already using two spoken languages at home.

Are you using two or more languages at home? If you're raising a bilingual baby, you might be wondering how signing does—or doesn't—fit in with your communication.

You will find that signing can provide an incredible tool to support your baby's language development in a multilingual home. When your child sees the same sign paired with words in both languages, it's a powerful and organic visual clue that the spoken words mean the same thing.

Here's one way to think about it: If somebody said "dog" to you and held up a photo of a dog, that would make sense to you. Now, if that person held up the same photo while saying "dog" in a language you didn't know, you would instantly know what that new word means, right? In a very similar way, baby sign language provides a visual prompt when paired with related words in multiple languages. The result? Signing makes it easier, not harder, for your baby to learn multiple spoken languages.

In a bilingual or multilingual home, baby signing can provide important information about how much your baby understands across languages. For example, if you ask your baby in English, "Do you want to eat?" and your baby signs **EAT** in response, you can feel confident that they understand you. If you ask your baby the same question in your second language and they also sign **EAT**, then you have a measure of validation that they are comprehending the question in both languages.

Does it matter which hand I use? What if my hands are full?

As a busy parent, you've always got your hands full, physically and metaphorically. Parents often ask if it matters which hand they sign with or what they should do if one or both of their hands are full. Here are some guidelines and tips to help you navigate this unique "handful" of a challenge.

In general, most signs are done with your dominant hand—the hand you write with. There are three general types of signs: one-handed signs, two-handed signs where the hands mirror each other, and two-handed signs where the hands are different.

For one-handed signs (like **MILK** and **EAT**), you simply sign with your dominant hand. For two-handed signs where the hands mirror each other (like **MORE** and **ALL DONE**), both hands do the same thing. But for two-handed signs where the hands are doing different hand shapes and/or motions (like **HELP** and **MUSIC**), your dominant hand is your "action" hand and your nondominant hand is your "support" hand, providing a base for the main movement.

When you've got a baby or toddler to care for, you'll find there are times when your dominant hand is busy or just one hand is available. In these situations, it's okay to improvise and modify the signs as needed.

For example, if you're cradling your baby in your dominant arm, you can sign **MILK** with your nondominant hand so that your baby can see it. Or if you're pushing a shopping cart through the supermarket, you can sign **ALL DONE** with just one hand instead of two as you tell your baby you're "all done" shopping and it's time to go home. For a two-handed sign like **HELP,** you can use just the dominant hand—the one that is doing the action.

Will using too many signs overwhelm my baby?

If you're just getting started, begin with a handful of signs that you can use throughout each day. Your ideal group of starter signs should include a couple of useful signs (signs you can use throughout your daily routines) and a couple of playful signs (signs for objects of high interest for baby). Some examples of useful signs are **MILK, BED, EAT, MORE,** and **ALL DONE**. Examples of playful signs are **DOG, LIGHT, BALL, BOOK,** and **CAR**.

After you've gotten the hang of signing and feel comfortable using the starter signs you've chosen, it's time to keep going and add a few more. How quickly you add more signs depends on your baby's age and your own comfort level. It might feel right to add a new sign every week or maybe even multiple signs in one day, depending on how quickly your baby is picking them up! Do what feels right when deciding to introduce more or hold off.

I typically recommend starting small and building with time. As a result, parents sometimes wonder if this recommendation is meant to avoid overwhelming the baby. Absolutely not! Babies learn language much more easily than adults. Their brains are primed to learn language, and they soak it up without effort. You absolutely do not need to worry about your baby being inundated with signs.

My recommendation to start small and build from there is more to keep you, the parent or caregiver, from getting overwhelmed. Chances are you're busy, tired, and maybe even sleep-deprived. I definitely don't want signing to feel like another chore on a seemingly endless to-do list!

Does everyone who spends time with my baby need to use sign language?

If you're taking the lead on introducing signs to your baby, you might be wondering how to get your partner or childcare provider on board with signing. You might be wondering, "If they don't also use signs, will it still work?"

The good news is, yes, you can still succeed with baby sign language, even if you're the only one teaching it to your little one. Of course, it would be ideal if all other caregivers used signs when caring for your baby, but that might not be practical or realistic for a variety of reasons. Just remember, it takes only one person to introduce baby sign language into your child's life.

Once your baby starts signing back, you will need to let others know what their signs look like and what they mean. This can be as simple as an email or a note that says something like "When Lily swings her arm from side to side, she is telling you that she is 'all done.'"

I have always enjoyed having grandparents in my signing classes. I've learned from them that often grandparents as well as partners and caregivers who originally weren't interested in signing become huge fans of the technique once they see it in action and experience the benefits of early communication. All it takes is one *Wow!* moment and they're on board.

How can I get my baby to do the signs correctly?

Say you've been signing **MORE** (touching fingers to thumbs and then tapping fingertips of both hands together) diligently every time you offer your baby more food or more pushes on the swing. It's been a few months now and your baby has started clapping their hands together when you ask if they want "more" to eat. Are they enthusiastic or are they signing?

Sometimes it can be hard to tell if your baby is signing to communicate or just clapping or waving, as babies often do. This is because their motor skills are still developing, and your baby simply doesn't have the fine and gross motor skills to sign with precision and accuracy just yet.

Just like those early spoken words, you'll find that early signs are your baby's best attempt at communicating. Your baby might call you "muh muh" or "dah dah" first. Similarly, your baby might clap or bang their fists together before signing **MORE** with the correct hand shape.

These early attempts at both spoken words and signs are called *approximations*, and they represent your baby's best attempt at their developmental stage. You don't need to worry about or even try to correct them. They are completely normal and appropriate and should be expected.

There is no need to "fix" your baby's hands. The truth is, doing so might actually frustrate your baby and undermine all the good work you're doing to teach them to sign. When you see your baby attempting to sign, simply acknowledge and respond to your little one's sign approximation and continue modeling the sign correctly. With time, you'll see your child's skills evolve and their signing become increasingly accurate. Just relax and enjoy the process! Years later, you'll think back nostalgically at those adorable "mistakes."

Why is my baby using the same sign for everything?
Why did my baby stop signing?

Your baby has started using sign language to communicate. Hooray! For some folks, once their little one begins to sign, it's smooth sailing. But for others there might be some speed bumps along the road.

The first potential speed bump is that once your baby starts signing, they use one sign all the time. This can be both confusing and frustrating! Your baby signs **MILK** all day long. Are they really hungry?

Think about it: As exciting as your baby's first sign is for you, it is even more exciting for your baby. They've just realized they have the power to use their tiny hands to communicate, and they want to use it! This is usually just a passing phase, so hang in there and continue to acknowledge your baby's communication. If your baby is signing **MILK** and you know they are not hungry, let them know you see their sign but take the opportunity to introduce a new one. You can say, "I see you signing **MILK** and we just had some **MILK**. Should we listen to some **MUSIC** now?"

Another equally confounding case is when your baby has been using a sign consistently to communicate and then, out of the blue, just stops using it for no apparent reason. What gives?

Your baby might have a lot going on right now, developmentally. Sometimes when babies are working on other developmental milestones, like cruising or walking, they might drop signing temporarily to focus their energy on mastering a new skill. Discomfort from teething or sickness can also impact their signing activity. If your baby stops signing, just keep modeling the signs and know that it's just a phase. Tell yourself, "This, too, shall pass." It's easy to feel discouraged or frustrated when this happens, but stay the course and know that it won't be long before your baby picks it back up again.

PART 2

Activities, Games, and More!

Want to know the secret to baby sign language? It's simple: Make signing fun and engaging! So many parents focus on using signs only in daily routines with their baby—for example, signing **DIAPER** or **CLEAN** at each and every diaper change or signing **BED** every time they put their baby down to rest. That's helpful for reinforcement, but where's the fun in that?

If you want to get your baby motivated to communicate with you, you'll need to work with their interests in order to make signing something that is enjoyable and fun. In the following pages, I'll share 65 fun songs and games that you can use to capture your child's attention and get them interested in signing. With a simple song to sing and sign, even a diaper change can become something fun for you *and* baby, not just a repetitive chore.

This section of the book is composed of three chapters: Baby's Busy Day, Baby's Favorite Things, and Baby's Big World. In Baby's Busy Day, you'll learn songs and games to use throughout your daily routines. In Baby's Favorite Things, you'll learn fun activities for all the things your little one can't wait to discuss with you. And last, in Baby's Big World, you'll pick up songs and games to introduce more advanced vocabulary and concepts to your growing toddler. Let's get started!

CHAPTER 3

Baby's Busy Day

Taking care of young children involves many repetitive tasks throughout the day. Diaper changes, meals, and sleeping happen on a seemingly endless loop! It's no wonder parents and caregivers who focus on using signs during these mundane tasks often fail to ignite the spark required for baby sign language to succeed.

But there is a solution! Make everyday tasks and routines *fun*. There's no reason that getting dressed or having a snack must be dull! Adding a song with signs or a playful game can make bath time feel more like playtime.

In this chapter, you'll learn lots of fun ways to introduce starter signs to your little one in a playful way. You'll also learn how to make every-day activities, like diaper changes, meals, bedtime, and bath time, a fun language-building opportunity by adding signs to your routines. Use the repetitive nature of daily routines to your advantage! Incorporating songs and games into daily tasks provides loads of opportunities to teach your baby signs in a way that you'll both enjoy.

Mirror, Mirror

Babies are fascinated by mirrors. They love to look at themselves and at the reflection of their favorite person (that's you!), too. Spend a little time with your baby looking at your reflections in the mirror and use this time to teach them some useful signs as well.

WHAT YOU NEED
Wall-mounted or handheld mirror

HOW-TO
Sit with your baby in front of a mirror where you can both see your reflections.

Smile and wave to your baby. Say, "I see **YOU**!" and point to your baby in the mirror.

Ask your baby, "Who is that? Is that my **BABY**?" while pointing to their reflection.

Say, "I see **MOMMY**!" and then point to yourself or touch your own reflection.

KEY VOCABULARY

YOU - Point index finger away from self

BABY - Cradle your arms and rock them side to side

MOM - Tap thumb of open hand on chin

DAD - Tap thumb of open hand on forehead

Handy Tip: Keep items nearby for which you'd like to introduce signs (like a book or a cup of water) and take advantage of your baby's focus on the mirror to introduce additional signs.

Skidamarink

This sweet little song is the perfect way to let your baby know just how much you love them. It's also the perfect way to teach your baby the signs for **I, LOVE,** and **YOU**. You can sign and sing this song in an energetic and playful way during the day or in a quiet, soothing way at night.

Skidamarink a-dink a-dink
Skidamarink a-doo
I LOVE YOU

Oh, skidamarink a-dink a-dink
Skidamarink a-doo
I LOVE YOU

I love you (sign **I-L-Y**) in the morning
And in the afternoon
I love you (sign **I-L-Y**) in the evening
And underneath the moon

KEY VOCABULARY

I - Touch index finger to chest **LOVE** - Cross arms over chest **YOU** - Point index finger away from self **I-L-Y** - Bend two middle fingers down

Handy Tip: In the second verse, use the ASL sign for **I-L-Y** as a shorthand way to say "I love you."

What's Inside?

Babies love to put things in and take things out of containers. Make this a fun game by placing a "mystery" object inside a container and shaking it to get your baby's attention. Use a bunch of different stuff to keep your baby guessing!

WHAT YOU NEED

A variety of small, baby-safe objects to place inside

Empty tissue box or wipes tub

HOW-TO

Place a small toy (like a rubber duck or a toy car) in the box.

Rattle the box gently so it gets your baby's attention.

Say to your baby, "**WHAT** do you think is inside? Shall we take it **OUT**?" Use your voice in addition to signs to express curiosity and excitement for the activity.

Offer the container to your baby to let them explore and try to retrieve the toy on their own.

Offer to help get the object out if they are having trouble by saying, "It looks like you need some **HELP** getting it out. Do you want me to **HELP** you?"

Express excitement when you discover what was inside! "Look! It's a **DUCK**! Quack, quack, quack [sign **DUCK**]. Can you sign **DUCK**?"

Invite your baby to put the object back **IN** the container.

Repeat with a toy **CAR** or any other objects that represent words and signs you'd like to teach your little one.

continued

KEY VOCABULARY

WHAT - Hold palms up and shake side to side

OUT - Pull fingertips out of opposite curved hand

HELP - Place "thumbs up" hand on palm and lift

DUCK - Open and close two fingers to thumb at mouth

IN - Place fingertips inside opposite curved hand

CAR - Move closed fists up and down alternately

Handy Tip: If you don't have an empty tissue box or wipes container handy, a recycled gift bag is a great alternative. You can use multiple gift bags to make it even more fun, colorful, and exciting.

Apples and Bananas

This classic children's song provides the perfect opportunity to introduce and practice the sign for **EAT** (page 42) at mealtime. You can sing about "Apples and Bananas," or other foods like **PEAS** and **CARROTS,** or **CHEESE** (page 42) and **CRACKERS** (page 42).

LYRICS

I like to **EAT, EAT, EAT APPLES** and **BANANAS**

I like to **EAT, EAT, EAT APPLES** and **BANANAS**

I like to **EAT, EAT, EAT CHEESE** and **CRACKERS**

I like to **EAT, EAT, EAT CHEESE** and **CRACKERS**

I like to **EAT, EAT, EAT PEAS** and **CARROTS**

I like to **EAT, EAT, EAT PEAS** and **CARROTS**

KEY VOCABULARY

APPLE - Twist knuckle on cheek

BANANA - Move fingertips down opposite index finger

PEAS - Tap index finger along opposite index finger

CARROT - Hold fist next to mouth and move downward

Handy Tip: The song's original version plays with vowel sounds, which is great for phonemic awareness (understanding the sounds in spoken language). If you'd like to play with the spoken word for "eat" in additional verses of the song, you can pair the sign **EAT** with "ate," "ite," "ote," and "oot."

Blanket Swing

Older babies and toddlers love this game and usually want to do it again and again. Highly motivating activities like this are very effective to encourage your little one to sign. Enjoy your little one's delight as they experience the fun of playing with you!

WHAT YOU NEED

Small, sturdy blanket or quilt

Another adult (not recommended with older siblings or children)

HOW-TO

Lay a small blanket on a carpeted area, and ask your baby if they want to **SWING** on the **BLANKET**.

Lay your baby down in the center of the blanket.

Have your adult helper stand at your baby's head and hold two corners of the blanket while you hold the two corners at your baby's feet.

Together, lift your baby a few inches off the floor and gently rock from side to side. Make sure they are well supported and that you can see their face at all times.

Gently lower your baby to the floor and ask, "Do you want to swing **MORE**?"

If your baby is enjoying the game, repeat the previous steps. In time, your baby will sign **MORE** to let you know they want to continue.

When you or your baby have had enough of this game, say, "That was so fun, but now we're **ALL DONE**! Bye-bye, **BLANKET**!"

SWING - Place two bent fingers on opposite two fingers and swing

BLANKET - Pull closed hands upward on chest

MORE - Tap fingertips together twice

ALL DONE - Twist open hands away from you

Handy Tip: Some babies who've been taught only a few signs (like **MORE**) tend to overuse it because it's the only sign they know. Teaching the sign for **SWING** or **BLANKET** will allow your baby to specifically request this activity.

The More We Get Together

"The More We Get Together" is the perfect song to teach your baby the sign for **MORE**. Sing and sign this tune often, and your baby will have ample opportunities to hear and see the word *more* in both English and ASL. Don't forget to use the sign for **MORE** in a variety of contexts, so in addition to using it in the song, sign it when offering your baby more food or more pushes in the swing.

The **MORE** we get together

Together, together

The **MORE** we get together

The happier (sign **HAPPY**) we'll be

'Cause your **FRIENDS** are my **FRIENDS**

And my **FRIENDS** are your **FRIENDS**

The **MORE** we get together

The happier (sign **HAPPY**) we'll be

KEY VOCABULARY

MORE - Tap finger-tips together twice

HAPPY - Brush hand upward on chest

FRIEND - Hook bent index fingers, then switch

Handy Tip: In ASL, facial expression is important, especially when signing about emotions. When you sign **HAPPY**, your facial expression should match the sign with a happy expression.

Baby Doll's Bath Time

Enjoy outdoor water play on a hot day, or keep busy inside on a rainy day, with this activity. Toddlers long for autonomy, and this activity allows them to take on the grown-up role. It's baby doll's bath time, and your toddler needs to help!

WHAT YOU NEED

Plastic bin to serve as a bathtub
Waterproof baby doll
Washcloth

Soap
Bath toys
Towel

HOW-TO

Fill a plastic bin with lukewarm water. You can also do this outside if the weather is nice. Of course, never leave your child unattended near water.

Tell your toddler that it's time for the doll to take a **BATH**, and help them undress it and place it in the tub.

Prompt your toddler to use the washcloth and **SOAP** to scrub the **DOLL**. Encourage them to rinse the **DOLL** with water to get it nice and **CLEAN**.

Ask your baby if the **DOLL** wants to play in the tub. Show your baby the bath toys and ask, "Do you think the **DOLL** wants to play with the **BOAT** or the **DUCK**?" If your baby reaches for one of the toys, say, "Oh, you chose the **BOAT**! The **DOLL** wants to play with the **BOAT** in the tub."

Let your baby know when bath time is over, and invite them to **CLEAN** and dry the doll in a nice warm **TOWEL**.

continued

KEY VOCABULARY

BATH - Scrub fists on chest

SOAP - Brush fingers on opposite palm

DOLL - Slide bent index finger down nose twice

CLEAN - Slide flat hand along opposite palm

BOAT - Cupped hands move away in bouncing motion

DUCK - Open and close two fingers to thumb at mouth

TOWEL - Hold fists at shoulders and move side to side

DIRTY - Place hand under chin and wiggle fingers

Handy Tip: Smear some pudding or yogurt on the doll to show how "dirty" it is. Say, "Oh, goodness, this doll is so **DIRTY**! We'd better give her a **BATH** right away and get her all **CLEAN**!"

Good Morning, Good Night

Singing a simple song as part of your daily routine is a wonderful way to incorporate fun and easy language-building activities into your day. This tune can be sung cheerfully as you greet your baby each morning or in a quiet, gentle way as you wind down before bedtime. You can use all the signs below or just a few—whatever feels right to you.

LYRICS (SUNG TO THE TUNE OF "GOOD NIGHT, LADIES" FROM *THE MUSIC MAN*)

GOOD MORNING, **BABY**
GOOD MORNING, **BABY**
GOOD MORNING, **BABY**
It's time to start our day

GOOD NIGHT, **BABY**
GOOD NIGHT, **BABY**
GOOD NIGHT, **BABY**
It's time to go to sleep

KEY VOCABULARY

GOOD - Move your flat hand from chin to opposite palm

MORNING - Move hand upward from under opposite arm

BABY - Cradle your arms and rock them side to side

NIGHT - Bring bent hand down over back of opposite hand

Handy Tip: Babies love to hear their name! Alternate singing your baby's name instead of "baby" to make this song special and just for them.

Brush, Brush, Brush Your Teeth

Teeth can cause a lot of trouble in the first few years of life. Because of sensitive gums and new teeth, brushing teeth may not be your baby's favorite part of the day. But it's so important to keep those baby teeth clean and cavity-free. This simple and fun song will help you and baby get those teeth brushed and maybe even have fun in the process.

LYRICS (SUNG TO THE TUNE OF "ROW, ROW, ROW YOUR BOAT")

Brush, brush, brush your teeth
(sign **BRUSH TEETH**)

Make them nice and **WHITE**

Brush and scrub and scrub and brush
(sign **BRUSH TEETH**)

Now your smile is bright!

KEY VOCABULARY

BRUSH TEETH - Move index finger in front of teeth

WHITE - Move open hand off chest while closing fingers

Handy Tip: Have two toothbrushes on hand—one for you and one for your baby. Let your baby start by brushing their own teeth while you sing, then it's your turn to brush (and make sure they're really clean) while continuing the song.

Pick Me Up!

Some days it feels like your baby wants to be held all day long. Sometimes babies will even raise their open arms toward you and fuss to get their point across. Wouldn't it be nice if your baby used sign language instead of fussing? That's why you're here!

HOW-TO

Stand next to your little one and ask, "Do you want **UP**?" Give them a moment to respond before picking them up.

Next, say, "Daddy needs to put you **DOWN** now. I'm going to put you **DOWN**." Then return baby to the floor.

KEY VOCABULARY

UP - Move index
finger upward

DOWN - Move index
finger downward

Handy Tip: If your home has stairs, you can teach your baby the signs for **UP** and **DOWN** while using the stairs. Hold your baby and say, "Do you want to go **UP** the stairs?" and then take a few steps up. Ask again and again until you reach the top. Repeat the same for going down the stairs.

Change Your Diaper

Diaper changes happen many times throughout the day, so it's a great time to incorporate signing into your routine. Also, diaper changes usually provide good eye contact while your baby is up on a changing table, closer to your face. Singing a simple song as part of your routine will make diaper changes predictable for your baby, something little ones crave.

CHANGE your **DIAPER**

CHANGE your **DIAPER**

CHANGE your **DIAPER**

'Cause it's **WET**

I am gonna **CHANGE** your **DIAPER**

So you will be nice and **CLEAN**

KEY VOCABULARY

CHANGE - Stack closed fists and rotate positions

DIAPER - Open and close two fingers to thumbs at hips

WET - Open palms up and move downward, closing fingers

CLEAN - Slide flat hand along opposite palm

Handy Tip: The sign for **DIAPER** is done at the hips, which is difficult for baby to see. Babies naturally focus on their parent's or caregiver's face, so move your hands up higher—at your chest, for example—when signing **DIAPER** so your baby can see it. Another option is to use the sign for **CHANGE** instead of **DIAPER**.

The Handwashing Song

Learning to wash hands thoroughly is an important life skill for toddlers to practice. Once your little one starts exploring the world with their hands, it becomes important to wash hands frequently throughout the day to avoid germs and illness, especially since young children are often putting their hands in their mouths. Create good handwashing habits and hygiene by washing your and your baby's hands before every meal and snack. You can make handwashing fun with this simple song. Say to your baby, "Okay, it's time to wash our hands [sign **WASH HANDS**] because they're **DIRTY**! Let's go to the sink and get your hands nice and **CLEAN**!" If you're out of the house and on the go, you can use this song when using disposable hand wipes or water-free hand cleaner to clean your baby's hands.

LYRICS (SUNG TO THE TUNE OF "FRÈRE JACQUES")

Top and bottom, top and bottom
(sign **WASH HANDS**)

In between, in between

Scrub and make some bubbles, scrub and make some bubbles

Wash your hands, wash your hands
(sign **WASH HANDS**)

Top and bottom, top and bottom
(sign **WASH HANDS**)

In between, in between

Scrub and make some bubbles, scrub and make some bubbles

Now they're **CLEAN**, squeaky **CLEAN**

continued

The Handwashing Song continued

WASH HANDS - Rub
hands together

DIRTY - Place hand
under chin and
wiggle fingers

CLEAN - Slide
flat hand along
opposite palm

Handy Tip: Sing this song as you're washing your own hands so your baby will begin to associate it with the activity. Babies are careful observers and are eager to do all the same things they see you doing.

My Family

Babies love looking at faces. Research has shown that babies start to recognize familiar faces as early as two months old. By creating a photo album of close friends and family members, you'll satisfy their desire to look at faces and also help them identify loved ones. Our baby's photo album was well used and is now a treasured keepsake.

WHAT YOU NEED

Soft, baby-friendly photo album (search for "baby's first photo album" if shopping online)

Photos of friends, caregivers, and family members

HOW-TO

Make sure the photos are cropped closely to show faces, like a headshot or school portrait, before printing.

Flip through the album with your baby and say each person's name as you point at their photo. Say, "Oh, look at this photo of **GRANDMA. GRANDMA** loves you so much!" Do the same for **MOMMY** (page 19), **DADDY** (page 19)**, SISTER, BROTHER, AUNT,** or **UNCLE**.

You can pair family signs with the name (or title) you use for your relatives. For example, pair the sign for **GRANDPA** with "papa" or the sign for **GRANDMA** with "abuela" if that's the name you use.

You can pair the sign for **TEACHER** with the childcare teacher's name or the sign for **BABYSITTER** with the name of your nanny. **FRIEND** (page 26) is a great sign to use for important people in your baby's life who don't have a specific relation or title.

continued

KEY VOCABULARY

GRANDMA - Bounce open hand away from chin twice

SISTER - Move *L* hand from chin to opposite *L* hand

BROTHER - Move *L* hand from forehead to opposite *L* hand

AUNT - Circle *A* hand near jawline

UNCLE - Circle *U* hand near temple

GRANDPA - Bounce open hand away from forehead twice

TEACHER - Closed fingertips move away from temples, then flat hands downward

BABYSITTER - Stack *K* hands, then tap or move in circular motion

Handy Tip: Babies enjoy the tactile experience of flipping through a photo album. If you don't have time to print photos, you can create a digital photo album for baby to see on your phone or tablet.

Good Night, House

Transitioning from playtime to bedtime can be tough for busy babies. There are just so many fun things to do! Taking a stroll through your home and saying "good night" to familiar items can be a calming ritual as you move from the main area of your home to where your baby sleeps. Think of it as your own customized version of the classic board book *Goodnight Moon* by Margaret Wise Brown.

HOW-TO

Let your baby know it's time to begin your bedtime routine. Say, "It's time to say good night to the **HOUSE**. Can you **HELP** (page 22) me say good night to everything?"

Pick your baby up and start where you are. The idea is to start with the more exciting things (like your baby's favorite **TOYS**) and move toward less interesting things (like the **TABLE** or the **CHAIR**).

As you move through the house, turn off the lights in each room, if possible. Say, "Good night, **LIGHTS**." With older babies and toddlers, allow them to flip the light switch off, if possible.

Stop by a window and say good night to the **SKY** or the **MOON** and **STARS.**

Babies love predictability, so try to do your good night walk through the house in the same order each night.

continued

KEY VOCABULARY

HOUSE - Touch fingertips of flat hands, move outward and down

TOY - Twist *T* hands away from each other

TABLE - Tap top forearm twice on lower forearm

CHAIR - Tap bent two fingers twice on opposite two fingers

LIGHT - Lift hand up and open fingers downward

SKY - Sweep arm over your head

MOON - Move curved fingers from cheek upward

STAR - Brush index fingers against each other over head

Handy Tip: As you walk through your home holding baby, you'll have only one hand available for signing, and that's okay! Modify two-handed signs to be one-handed in situations like this.

Twinkle, Twinkle, Little Star

Babies love this song and its familiar tune (which is the same melody as "Baa, Baa, Black Sheep" and the "ABC Song"). You can incorporate this song into your bedtime routine, perhaps at the end of your "Good Night, House" walk (page 37). If you already know some gestures to use along with the song, like opening your fingers upward when you sing "twinkle, twinkle," it's fine to combine those gestures with ASL signs. Gestures and signs both help support early communication skills, and gestures (like clapping, waving, and pointing) are fun and important, too.

LYRICS (SIMPLE VERSION)

Twinkle, twinkle, little **STAR**

How I wonder **WHAT** you are

Up above the world so high

Like a diamond in the sky

Twinkle, twinkle, little **STAR**

How I wonder **WHAT** you are

LYRICS (ADVANCED VERSION)

Twinkle, twinkle, **LITTLE STAR**

How I wonder **WHAT YOU** are

UP above the world so high

Like a diamond in the **SKY**

Twinkle, twinkle, **LITTLE STAR**

How I wonder **WHAT** you are

continued

KEY VOCABULARY

STAR - Brush index fingers against each other over head

WHAT - Hold palms up and shake side to side

LITTLE - Move open hands toward each other

YOU - Point index finger away from self

UP - Move index finger upward

SKY - Sweep arm over your head

Handy Tip: When you are first getting started with signing, it can sometimes feel overwhelming. I encourage you to start simple and grow from there. You can start by simply adding the sign for **STAR** to the song. Next, add the sign for **WHAT**. As your confidence and vocabulary grow, you'll feel more comfortable adding more signs to the song.

Snack Surprise

Once your baby is big enough to feed themselves, there's a whole world of flavors and textures to discover. Offering your baby a variety of foods helps them explore their preferences and gain exposure to different tastes. By teaching your little one the signs for specific foods, they'll be able to let you know exactly what they want, instead of fussing and reaching to communicate.

WHAT YOU NEED

Muffin tin

A variety of small snacks and finger
   foods safe for baby

Sticky notes

HOW-TO

Fill each cup of the muffin tin with bite-size pieces of food. Include a variety of flavors (sweet and savory) and textures (crunchy and soft). Some suggestions are cut grapes, blueberries, raisins, small crackers, O-shaped cereal, and small bites of cheese.

Cover each section of the muffin tin with a sticky note and encourage your toddler to peek under one. Ask, "Did you find something to **EAT**? **WHAT** is it?"

As baby explores the muffin tin, talk about the food and demonstrate the sign. Say, "Yum, that's a blueberry [sign **BERRY**]! Do you like blueberries [sign **BERRY**]?"

Try not to make a big deal about your baby's reaction to each food. If your baby spits out a food, simply say, "You don't want that **CHEESE** right now. Maybe another time."

Repeat this for each of the foods, commenting on the flavor and texture of each one.

continued

KEY VOCABULARY

EAT - Tap fingertips to mouth

WHAT - Hold palms up and shake side to side

BERRY - Twist fingertips on opposite index finger

CHEESE - Twist palms against each other

GRAPES - Tap fingertips down opposite wrist and hand

RAISINS - Sign *R* and tap down opposite wrist and hand

CEREAL - Wiggle index finger across chin

CRACKER - Knock fist on opposite elbow

Handy Tip: EAT and **MORE** (page 25) are very useful signs, but teaching your baby the specific signs for favorite foods will allow them to communicate more clearly and precisely.

Baby Shark

If you've got a toddler, there's just no escaping the song "Baby Shark"! Little ones love the catchy and repetitive tune, so embrace it and have fun. It also happens to be the perfect song to teach your baby the signs for **MOM, DAD, GRANDMA,** and **GRANDPA**, so use their love of "Baby Shark" to show them some useful ASL vocabulary!

LYRICS

BABY SHARK, doo doo doo doo doo doo

BABY SHARK, doo doo doo doo doo doo

BABY SHARK, doo doo doo doo doo doo

BABY SHARK!

MOMMY SHARK, doo doo doo doo doo doo

MOMMY SHARK, doo doo doo doo doo doo

MOMMY SHARK, doo doo doo doo doo doo

MOMMY SHARK!

DADDY SHARK, doo doo doo doo doo doo . . .

GRANDMA SHARK, doo doo doo doo doo doo . . .

GRANDPA SHARK, doo doo doo doo doo doo . . .

Let's go **PLAY**, doo doo doo doo doo doo

Let's go **PLAY**, doo doo doo doo doo doo

Let's go **PLAY**, doo doo doo doo doo doo

Let's go **PLAY**!

continued

KEY VOCABULARY

BABY - Cradle your arms and rock them side to side

SHARK - Hold your *B* hand at your forehead

MOM - Tap thumb of open hand on chin

DAD - Tap thumb of open hand on forehead

GRANDMA - Bounce open hand away from chin twice

GRANDPA - Bounce open hand away from forehead twice

PLAY - Twist *Y* hands away from each other

Handy Tip: This is a fun song to get your wiggles out to! Dance and "swim" around like a baby shark while singing and signing along to this playful and energetic tune.

Fashion Show

It's so fun for toddlers to try on Mommy's sunglasses or put their feet in Daddy's big shoes. Little ones love to play dress-up, which makes it the perfect time to build vocabulary. The sillier you can make it, the more fun this activity will be. Ask your child to put on one of your **SHIRTS** to see if it fits. Or better yet, see if you can get your foot into one of your toddler's little **SHOES** (page 46)—that's sure to get a laugh!

WHAT YOU NEED

A variety of clothing items (hats, scarves, sunglasses, shirts, shoes) in a mix of sizes

bin or laundry basket

HOW-TO

Collect a wide variety of clothing items in a bin or laundry basket and place it on the floor where your baby can reach.

As your baby pulls each item out, name the item and model the sign for it. Say, "Oh, look, you found Mommy's **HAT**! Do you want to try it on?" Then say, "Oh, no, it's too **BIG** (page 52)!"

Take a shoe from the basket and place it on your own head. Ask your toddler, "Is this a

HAT? Do you like Daddy's **HAT**?" Your toddler might take the shoe from your head because they know it doesn't belong there. Say, "That's not a **HAT**, that's a **SHOE**! Daddy is so **SILLY** (page 102)!"

If your child is having a difficult time putting an item of clothing on themselves, ask, "Do you need some **HELP** putting that on?"

continued

KEY VOCABULARY

SHIRT - Pinch and pull your shirt slightly

HAT - Pat your head

SHOES - Knock closed fists together

HELP - Place "thumbs up" hand on palm and lift

PANTS - Slide flat hands down sides of each thigh

SOCKS - Brush index fingers against each other pointing down

COAT - Slide fists from shoulders down torso

CLOTHES - Brush thumbs of open hand down chest

Handy Tip: You can use the sign for **CLOTHES**, which also means "get dressed," when telling your child it's time to get dressed.

Grocery Store

There's a reason play kitchens are so popular with toddlers: They provide many fun activities for babies, like opening and closing doors and drawers. Take your toddler's interest to the next level by setting up a play grocery store for them to shop in. Your child will be delighted by the chance to shop the available options, and it's a great time to introduce and practice signs for foods, too.

WHAT YOU NEED

A variety of canned, boxed, and fresh food (you can use toy food if you prefer)

Coffee table and/or bookshelves

Laundry basket ("grocery cart")

Disposable or reusable shopping bags

A library card or other plastic card

HOW-TO

Place real or play food items on a low table or shelves. Group similar items together (like cans and boxes) as you would see them at the grocery store.

Tell your toddler it's time to go to the **STORE** to get lots of things to **EAT** (page 42).

Model "shopping" by putting items in your grocery cart, and encourage your little one to continue shopping. Ask, "Should we get some **FRUIT**? Or maybe some **YOGURT**?"

Once your child has finished shopping, check out. You can be the cashier! Have your toddler use a library or membership card as their credit card to pay for their groceries.

Have your toddler help you place the items in bags to bring home to the kitchen and put away.

continued

KEY VOCABULARY

STORE - Close fingers to thumbs and flick outward twice

FRUIT - Twist *F* hand next to mouth

YOGURT - Move *Y* hand from curved hand to mouth

MILK - Squeeze your hand open and closed

PASTA - Spiral *I* hands away from each other

COOKIE - Tap and twist fingertips on opposite palm

BREAD - Slide fingertips down back of other hand

VEGETABLES - Twist *V* hand next to mouth

Handy Tip: There are a lot of signs to choose from for this activity, like **MILK, PASTA, COOKIES, BREAD, VEGETABLES,** and **YOGURT**. Don't get overwhelmed. Use as many or as few as you like, or add some more each time you play.

Five Little Monkeys

This is a fun and energetic song that also features really practical signs, like **BED, HURT, DOCTOR,** and **NO**. You'll see in the lyrics how you can progressively add more signs to the song as your comfort and skills with signing grow. In the first verse, there is just one sign per line. In each subsequent verse, I've added another sign or two. You can also add the ASL signs for the numbers 1 through 5, which you can find on page xii.

LYRICS

Five little **MONKEYS** jumping on the bed,

One fell off and bumped (sign **HURT**) his head.

MAMA called the doctor and the doctor said,

"No more **MONKEYS** jumping on the bed."

Four little **MONKEYS** jumping on the **BED**,

One fell off and bumped (sign **HURT**) his head.

MAMA called the doctor and the doctor said,

"No more **MONKEYS** jumping on the **BED**."

Three little **MONKEYS** jumping on the **BED**,

One fell off and bumped (sign **HURT**) his head.

MAMA called the **DOCTOR** and the **DOCTOR** said,

"No more **MONKEYS** jumping on the **BED**."

Two little **MONKEYS** jumping on the **BED**,

One fell off (sign **FALL DOWN**) and bumped (sign **HURT**) his head.

MAMA called the **DOCTOR** and the **DOCTOR** said,

"**NO** more **MONKEYS** jumping on the **BED**."

ONE little **MONKEY** jumping on the **BED**,

He fell off (sign **FALL DOWN**) and bumped (sign **HURT**) his head.

MAMA called (sign **PHONE**) the **DOCTOR** and the **DOCTOR** said,

"Put those **MONKEYS** straight to **BED**."

continued

KEY VOCABULARY

MONKEY - Scratch
your sides

HURT - Point index
fingers at each other

MOM - Tap thumb of
open hand on chin

BED - Tilt head onto
open hand

DOCTOR - Tap three
fingers on inside of
opposite wrist

FALL DOWN - Move
inverted *V* hand
sideways and down
from palm

NO - Open and close
two fingers to thumb
at shoulder

PHONE - Tap *Y* hand
to side of head

Bubble Fun

Bubbles are a fun, super-motivating, and perfect opportunity to teach your baby to request **MORE**. They can be used outdoors on a nice day or in the bathroom to kick bath time up a notch. In this activity, you'll learn a variety of ways to play with bubbles and teach your baby some signs, too!

WHAT YOU NEED
Bubble solution or dish soap
Bubble wands of various sizes (or drinking straws and cardboard tubes)

Plastic bin
A whisk or slotted spoon

HOW-TO

You can buy premade bubble solution (which usually comes with a wand), or you can make your own with ¼ cup of liquid dish soap and ¾ cup of water.

When your baby is playing in the bathtub, blow bubbles over their head and say, "Look at the **BUBBLES**!" Your baby will likely reach and try to touch the bubbles, causing them to pop. When the bubbles are gone, ask, "Do you want **MORE BUBBLES**?" If you baby isn't signing yet but shows excitement for more, say, "You want **MORE BUBBLES**! Let's blow **MORE BUBBLES**."

Fill a bin with ¾ water and ¼ liquid dish soap. Use a whisk or slotted spoon to whip up some frothy bubbles. Talk about how there are so many **BUBBLES** and encourage your toddler to stir the froth and make **MORE**.

Blow small bubbles with a small wand or drinking straw and comment on how **SMALL** the bubbles are. Then blow bubbles with a larger wand or an empty paper towel tube and comment on how **BIG** the bubbles are. Ask your toddler if they want more **BIG** or **SMALL BUBBLES**.

continued

KEY VOCABULARY

MORE - Tap finger-tips together twice

BUBBLES - Make circles with fingers and open them alternately

SMALL - Move open hands toward each other

BIG - Move open hands away from each other

Handy Tip: Use your voice to help convey the difference between **BIG** and **SMALL**! Use a deep voice when you say and sign **BIG**, and a high voice when you say and sign **SMALL**.

This Is the Way

You can use this simple tune for just about anything, especially when you're just not sure what to talk about. For instance, you can make getting your wiggly baby dressed a little easier and turn it into a learning opportunity. Hold an article of clothing up and say, "Here are your **SOCKS**. It's time to put your **SOCKS** on." Then sing the appropriate verse from the following tune as you put baby's socks on.

LYRICS (SUNG TO THE TUNE OF "HERE WE GO 'ROUND THE MULBERRY BUSH")

This is the way we put on our **PANTS**
Put on our **PANTS**, put on our **PANTS**
This is the way we put on our **PANTS**
When we're **GETTING DRESSED**

This is the way we put on our **SHIRT**
Put on our **SHIRT**, put on our **SHIRT**
This is the way we put on our **SHIRT**
When we're **GETTING DRESSED**

This is the way we put on our **SOCKS**
Put on our **SOCKS**, put on our **SOCKS**
This is the way we put on our **SOCKS**
When we're **GETTING DRESSED**

This is the way we put on our **SHOES**
Put on our **SHOES**, put on our **SHOES**
This is the way we put on our **SHOES**
When we're **GETTING DRESSED**

This is the way we put on our **HAT**
Put on our **HAT**, put on our **HAT**
This is the way we put on our **HAT**
When we're **GETTING DRESSED**

This is the way we put on our **COAT**
Put on our **COAT**, put on our **COAT**
This is the way we put on our **COAT**
When we're **GETTING DRESSED**

continued

KEY VOCABULARY

SOCKS - Brush index fingers against each other pointing down

PANTS - Slide flat hands down sides of each thigh

GET DRESSED - Brush thumbs of open hands down chest

SHIRT - Pinch and pull your shirt slightly

SHOES - Knock closed fists together

HAT - Pat your head

COAT - Slide fists from shoulders down torso

CHAPTER 4

Baby's Favorite Things

Want to know the secret to baby signing success? It's pretty simple: Choose and teach signs based on your child's interests! Always keep in mind that your baby will be more motivated to communicate with you about the things in their world that matter most to them, whether it's their favorite food, pet, or toy.

In this chapter, we'll focus on the vocabulary for various things babies and toddlers love the most. Incorporating signs for high-interest items, like animals, toys, and vehicles, will capture your baby's interest and make signing easier and more fun.

You'll learn how to play simple games using common household items (like pots and pans or a laundry basket) or toys you already have (like a teddy bear or a ball). You'll also learn how to add signs to songs you already know and love, like "Old MacDonald Had a Farm," "The Wheels on the Bus," and more. Let's play!

Five Green and Speckled Frogs

You and your little one will have so much fun singing and signing this song together! This is a crowd favorite with toddlers and preschoolers, in part because it's so silly and because it's so fun to pretend you're the frog enjoying those yummy bugs!

Five **GREEN** and speckled **FROGS**
SAT on a speckled log
EATING some most delicious **BUGS**
Yum, yum

One **JUMPED** into the pool
WHERE it was nice and cool
Then there were four **GREEN** speckled **FROGS**
Ribbit, ribbit (sign **FROG**)

Four **GREEN** and speckled **FROGS**
SAT on a speckled log
EATING some most delicious **BUGS**
Yum, yum

One **JUMPED** into the pool
WHERE it was nice and cool
Then there were three **GREEN** speckled **FROGS**
Ribbit, ribbit (sign **FROG**)

Three **GREEN** and speckled **FROGS**
SAT on a speckled log
EATING some most delicious **BUGS**
Yum, yum

One **JUMPED** into the pool
WHERE it was nice and cool
Then there were two **GREEN** speckled **FROGS**
Ribbit, ribbit (sign **FROG**)

Two **GREEN** and speckled **FROGS**
SAT on a speckled log
EATING some most delicious **BUGS**
Yum, yum

One **JUMPED** into the pool
WHERE it was nice and cool
Then there was one **GREEN** speckled **FROG**
Ribbit, ribbit (sign **FROG**)

continued

One **GREEN** and speckled **FROG**
SAT on a speckled log
EATING some most delicious **BUGS**
Yum, yum

He **JUMPED** into the pool
WHERE it was nice and cool
Then there were **NO GREEN**
speckled **FROGS**

KEY VOCABULARY

GREEN - Make *G* hand shape and shake

FROG - With fist under chin, pop two fingers out twice

SIT - Place two bent fingers on opposite two fingers

EAT - Tap fingertips to mouth

BUG - Thumb of "3" hand on nose and bend fingers twice

JUMP - Bend and lift inverted *V* fingers from palm

WHERE - Shake index finger side to side

NO - Open and close two fingers to thumb at shoulder

Toy Rescue

Oh, no, baby's toy is stuck inside the container! Your baby will be highly motivated to rescue their trapped toy and will turn learning valuable vocabulary into a fun game that they will want to play over and over. This game provides the opportunity to introduce a combination of both practical and playful sign language vocabulary.

WHAT YOU NEED

A variety of small toys

Clear plastic containers with lids (large enough to hold the toys)

HOW-TO

Place an object of interest (like a small toy or book) inside a clear storage container with a lid. You can do this with one toy and container or with multiple containers and toys.

Show your baby the container and give it a little shake. Say, "Oh, no! The **BALL** is stuck inside! Can you **HELP** me?" and give the container to your baby.

Your baby might also shake the container or bang on it. Ask your baby, "Do you need **HELP**? Do you want me to **OPEN** it and get your **BALL**?"

Take the lid off and let your child play with the toy and container. Say, "Hooray! We **OPENED** it and got your **BALL**!"

As your baby plays, they might put the toy back in the container and try to put the lid back on. You can narrate their actions for them by saying, "Oh, you want to put it back **IN** the box. You **CLOSED** the box. Do you want to take it **OUT**?"

continued

KEY VOCABULARY

HELP - Place "thumbs up" hand on palm and lift

BALL - Move "claw" hands toward each other

OPEN - *B* hands start palms down and lift up and outward

IN - Place finger-tips inside opposite curved hand

CLOSE - *B* hands start palms facing and move inward and down

OUT - Pull finger-tips out of opposite curved hand

Handy Tip: The objective of this activity is to have fun, not to frustrate your baby. Be sure to help your baby as needed to keep it enjoyable!

When Dogs Get Up in the Morning

If you have a pet, chances are your baby is fascinated with it. Teaching your little one the signs for pets will help them initiate conversations around topics of high interest to them. Plus, babies are highly motivated to learn these signs and tend to pick them up quickly. This simple song will help you practice pet signs and introduce the sounds that animals say.

LYRICS

When **DOGS** get up in the **MORNING**
They always say, "Good day!"
When **DOGS** get up in the **MORNING**
They always say, "Good day!"
NO, NO! That's not what they say!
Ruff, ruff, ruff, ruff (sign **DOG**)
That is what they say.

When **CATS** get up in the **MORNING**
They always say, "Good day!"
When **CATS** get up in the **MORNING**
They always say, "Good day!"
NO, NO! That's not what they say!
Meow, meow, meow, meow (sign **CAT**)
That is what they say.

When **BIRDS** get up in the **MORNING**
They always say, "Good day!"
When **BIRDS** get up in the **MORNING**
They always say, "Good day!"
NO, NO! That's not what they say!
Tweet, tweet, tweet, tweet (sign **BIRD**)
That is what they say.

When **FISH** get up in the **MORNING**
They always say, "Good day!"
When **FISH** get up in the **MORNING**
They always say, "Good day!"
NO, NO! That's not what they say!
Glub, glub, glub, glub (sign **FISH**)
That is what they say.

continued

KEY VOCABULARY

MORNING - Move hand upward from under opposite arm

DOG - Pat your thigh

CAT - Pinch fingers near cheek and move outward

BIRD - Open and close index finger and thumb at mouth

FISH - Move hand in swerving motion away from you

NO - Open and close two fingers to thumb at shoulder

Handy Tip: Animals sounds (like "moo") are generally easier to say than the name of the animal ("cow") itself. This is why toddlers often use animal sounds to identify animals when they first start to talk. Teach your baby animal sounds, in addition to signs, to help them communicate early.

Ball Fun!

Balls come in an endless variety of colors, sizes, and textures, and they are very versatile playtime toys. As busy parents and caregivers, you might not have time to set up elaborate crafts and activities, but with a simple ball, you can help your child develop language skills and gross motor skills—and connect with you, too!

WHAT YOU NEED

Rubber balls (a variety of sizes)
Plastic cups

Laundry basket
Couch cushions

HOW-TO

Sit on the floor facing your child and roll a ball to them. Say, "You got the **BALL**! Now roll the **BALL** to me. Hooray!"

Set up some lightweight plastic cups like bowling pins. Show your baby how to roll the ball to knock them over. Set them back up again and say, "Now it's your turn. Can you roll the **BALL** and knock them down?"

Place an empty laundry basket on the floor. Gently toss a ball into the basket. Say, "The **BALL** is **IN** the basket! Can you put the **BALL IN** the basket, too?"

Lean a couch cushion against the couch and roll a ball down the cushion and onto the floor. Sit with your baby on your lap or next to you with a stash of balls for rolling. Show your baby how to let the ball roll down and then let them try it. They'll probably want to do it again and again! When all the balls are on the floor, ask, "Do you want do it **AGAIN**? Can you **HELP** me get the **BALLS** so we can do it **AGAIN**?"

continued

KEY VOCABULARY

BALL - Move "claw" hands toward each other

IN - Place fingertips inside opposite curved hand

AGAIN - Fingertips flip to land on opposite palm

HELP - Place "thumbs up" hand on palm and lift

Clean Up Song

Playtime is fun, which makes it so hard to stop playing and clean up. Using a simple song can let your child know it's a transition time. By singing this song and giving your toddler a specific task, like putting the stuffed animals on the shelf, you can make the process more fun!

LYRICS (SUNG TO THE TUNE OF "MARY HAD A LITTLE LAMB")

We made a mess, it's time to **HELP**
CLEAN our mess, **CLEAN** our mess
We made a mess, it's time to **HELP**
Time to **CLEAN** up now

Put the **TOYS** and **BOOKS** away
BOOKS away, **BOOKS** away
We made a mess, it's time to **HELP**
Time to **CLEAN** up now

KEY VOCABULARY

HELP - Place "thumbs up" hand on palm and lift

CLEAN - Slide flat hand along opposite palm

TOY - Twist *T* hands away from each other

BOOK - Place flat hands together and open outward

Handy Tip: Once your child gets the hang of signing, you can use signs without speaking to communicate more discreetly. You can silently sign **CLEAN** or **THANK YOU** (page 108) to prompt your child in social situations when it's time to help out or show gratitude to a friend.

Teddy Bear's Birthday

Help your little one prepare for their upcoming birthday celebration or an older sibling's special day by throwing a pretend birthday party for their favorite stuffed animal. Pretend play is a great way to help your little one know what to expect in new situations, like a big family gathering or even a trip to the dentist.

WHAT YOU NEED

Teddy bear
Small toys and items

Gift wrap
Balloons and party hats

HOW-TO

Tell your child that today is teddy bear's **BIRTHDAY** and you're going to have a **PARTY**!

Wrap some small toys or household items in gift wrap or tinfoil. This is a great opportunity to teach your child new vocabulary, so if you've been wanting to introduce the sign for **BANANA** (page 23), then gift wrap a banana!

If you have party items, like **BALLOONS** and other decorations, put them up and talk to your baby about them.

Tell your child that **BIRTHDAYS** are special days when we celebrate and sometimes give presents.

Take a wrapped gift and ask your baby, "**WHAT** (page 22) do you think it is? Should we **OPEN** it?"

Open all the gifts, modeling the sign for each item as you do.

BIRTHDAY - Bent middle finger touches chin, then chest

PARTY - *P* hands swing side to side

BALLOON - Closed fists open and move apart

OPEN - *B* hands start palms down and lift up and outward

Handy Tip: Exchanging gifts is the perfect time to model saying **THANK YOU** (page 108). As adults, we're eager for our kids to demonstrate good manners, but these skills take years to develop. The best way to teach your child to say **PLEASE** (page 108) and **THANK YOU** is to sign and say them yourself. In time, your child will follow the positive example you have set.

Zoom, Zoom, Zoom

Teach your child the signs for **SUN, MOON,** and **STARS** with this playful song. Many children's books include illustrations of these objects, and teaching your baby these signs will allow them to "read along" to their favorite books.

LYRICS

Zoom, zoom, zoom
We're going to the **MOON**
Zoom, zoom, zoom
We're going to the **MOON**
If you want to take a trip
Climb aboard my **ROCKET** ship
Zoom, zoom, zoom
We're going to the **MOON**
In 5, 4, 3, 2, 1
Blast off! (sign **ROCKET**)

Far, far, far
We're going to the **STARS**
Far, far, far
We're going to the **STARS**
If you want to take a trip
Climb aboard my **ROCKET** ship
Far, far, far
We're going to the **STARS**

In 5, 4, 3, 2, 1
Blast off! (sign **ROCKET**)

Fun, fun, fun
We're going to the **SUN**
Fun, fun, fun
We're going to the **SUN**
If you want to take a trip
Climb aboard my **ROCKET** ship
Fun, fun, fun
We're going to the **SUN**
In 5, 4, 3, 2, 1
Blast off! (sign **ROCKET**)

MOON – Move curved fingers from cheek upward

ROCKET – *R* hand moves upward from opposite hand

STAR – Brush index fingers against each other over head

SUN – Draw circle with pointer, then open fingers downward

Dino Dig

Sensory play is great for your child's cognitive development as well as their emerging motor skills. Scooping and pouring dry beans will keep your little one busy while also providing language-building opportunities as they "excavate" buried treasures.

WHAT YOU NEED

Small toys (like dinosaurs, animals, cars, or trucks)
Plastic bin

5 pounds dry beans (any kind)
Measuring cups and large spoons

HOW-TO

Put some small toys in a plastic bin and cover them with the dry beans.

Place some measuring cups and large spoons around the edges of the bin.

As your baby begins to explore the contents of the bin, ask "**WHAT** do you think is in there?"

Ask your child, "**WHAT** did you find? Did you find a **DINOSAUR**? The **DINOSAUR** says, 'Roar!'"

When your child is done with the toy, bury it back under the dry beans and ask, "**WHERE** did it go?"

Tell your child, "I think there are some more **ANIMALS** hiding in there. Can you **HELP** me find them?"

Move the **CAR** or **TRUCK** over the top of the dry beans, exaggerating how bumpy it is. Say, "Oh my! This road is too bumpy for the **CAR**!"

Sit back and enjoy as your baby explores the textures and experiments with scooping and pouring. Narrate their actions to provide language for the activity.

WHAT - Hold palms up and shake side to side

DINOSAUR - Touch fingers to thumb and bob hand as it moves

WHERE - Shake index finger side to side

ANIMAL - Touch fingertips to front of shoulders and move elbows

HELP - Place "thumbs up" hand on palm and lift

CAR - Move closed fists up and down alternately

TRUCK - Move closed fists forward and backward alternately

Handy Tip: If your child tends to put things in their mouth, instead of beans you can use another edible alternative, like crumbled graham crackers or cereal. Simply place the graham crackers or cereal in a blender or food processor for a moment to make edible sand or dirt.

Hands-On Story Time

Reading books with your baby is one of the best ways to support their speech and language development. By signing along as you read, you allow your baby to be involved with the storytelling, too. You can make story time even more hands-on by providing props related to the book's vocabulary to help bring the story to life.

WHAT YOU NEED

Your baby's favorite board books

Items featured in the books (toy truck, stuffed bunny, etc.)

HOW-TO

Select a **BOOK**, perhaps *The Little Blue Truck*. Present a toy truck to your baby and model the sign for **TRUCK**. Say, "Look at this cute little **TRUCK**. Can you sign **TRUCK**? Beep, beep! Do you want to hold the **TRUCK** while I read to you?"

Read *Goodnight Moon* with your baby and offer a stuffed mouse or bunny for them to hold. As you read the book, point out the little **MOUSE** on each page or the **RABBIT** getting ready for bed.

KEY VOCABULARY

BOOK - Place flat hands together and open outward

TRUCK - Move closed fists forward and backward alternately

MOUSE - Brush tip of nose with index finger

RABBIT - Bend two fingers backward at the top of head

Five Little Monkeys Swinging in a Tree

This is a fun and cheeky song about some naughty monkeys who keep teasing poor Mr. Alligator. One by one, however, Mr. Alligator teaches the mischievous monkeys a lesson . . . until the last one, who learns he'd better leave Mr. Alligator alone!

LYRICS

Five little **MONKEYS** swinging in a **TREE**

Teasing Mr. **ALLIGATOR**

"You can't catch me! You can't catch me!"

Along came Mr. **ALLIGATOR**, as quiet as can be

And snapped (sign **ALLIGATOR**) that monkey right out of the **TREE**

Four little **MONKEYS** swinging in a **TREE**

Teasing Mr. **ALLIGATOR**

"You can't catch me! You can't catch me!"

Along came Mr. **ALLIGATOR**, as quiet as can be

And snapped (sign **ALLIGATOR**) that monkey right out of the **TREE**

Three little **MONKEYS** swinging in a **TREE**

Teasing Mr. **ALLIGATOR**

"You can't catch me! You can't catch me!"

Along came Mr. **ALLIGATOR**, as quiet as can be

And snapped (sign **ALLIGATOR**) that monkey right out of the **TREE**

Two little **MONKEYS** swinging in a **TREE**

Teasing Mr. **ALLIGATOR**

"You can't catch me! You can't catch me!"

Along came Mr. **ALLIGATOR**, as quiet as can be

And snapped (sign **ALLIGATOR**) that monkey right out of the **TREE**

continued

Five Little Monkeys Swinging in a Tree continued

One little **MONKEY** swinging in a **TREE**
Teasing Mr. **ALLIGATOR**
"You can't catch me! You can't catch me!"

Along came Mr. **ALLIGATOR**, as quiet as can be
And the **MONKEY** cried out, "Ha, ha! Missed me!"

KEY VOCABULARY

MONKEY - Scratch your sides

TREE - Twist open hand with elbow resting on opposite hand

ALLIGATOR - Open and close your "claw" hands

Handy Tip: If you do a big "snap" with your **ALLIGATOR** arms each time you sing "snapped," it's a very effective way to show how this sign represents a big, hungry alligator! And the exaggerated movement and sound is extra entertaining for baby.

Light Games

Babies are endlessly fascinated by lights, which they are naturally drawn to and are everywhere! Babies who learn the sign for **LIGHT** tend to use it often to share their excitement when they see lights on the ceiling, on appliances, in new places when you take baby out, and on some of their toys. Here are some fun ways to teach and practice the sign for **LIGHT**. This is an excellent way to get your baby interested in using signs to communicate!

WHAT YOU NEED

Flashlight

Some glowsticks

HOW-TO

Sit with your baby in a dim (but not dark) room. Shine the flashlight on items around the room and talk about what you see. Shine the light on the **BOOKS** on a shelf or on some **TOYS**.

Activate some glowsticks and hide them around a dimly lit room. Ask your toddler, "Can you find the **LIGHTS**? **WHERE** are they?" Then watch them find and collect the glowsticks. Make sure baby doesn't put them in their mouth.

KEY VOCABULARY

BOOK - Place flat hands together and open outward

TOY - Twist *T* hands away from each other

LIGHT - Lift hand up and open fingers downward

WHERE - Shake index finger side to side

Nursery Rhymes

While nursery rhymes might seem old-fashioned, they are a powerful tool to support your baby's language development. Rhyming words help your baby learn about word sounds in fun and repetitive ways, creating a strong foundation for preliteracy skills and, eventually, for learning to read. Adding sign language to nursery rhymes allows your baby to participate before they can say the words themselves.

LYRICS

Hickory dickory dock!

The **MOUSE** ran **UP** the clock.

The clock struck one,

The **MOUSE** ran **DOWN**,

Hickory, dickory, dock!

Little Miss Muffet, [sign **GIRL**]

SAT on a tuffet,

EATING (page 58) her curds and whey.

Along came a **SPIDER**,

Who **SAT** down beside her,

And frightened [sign **SCARED**] (page 102) Miss Muffet away.

Humpty Dumpty **SAT** on a wall,

Humpty Dumpty had a great **FALL** (page 50).

All the king's **HORSES** (page 86) and all the king's men

Couldn't put Humpty together **AGAIN** (page 64).

Oh, the grand old Duke of York,

He had ten thousand men,

He marched them **UP** to the top of the hill

And he marched them **DOWN** again.

And when they were **UP**, they were **UP**,

And when they were **DOWN**, they were **DOWN**,

And when they were only halfway **UP**,

They were neither **UP** nor **DOWN**.

Jack and Jill went **UP** the hill

To fetch a pail of **WATER**.

Jack **FELL DOWN** (page 50) and broke his crown

And Jill came tumbling after.

Little **BOY** Blue, come blow your horn,

The **SHEEP**'s (page 119) in the meadow, the **COW**'s (page 86) in the corn.

WHERE (page 58) is the **BOY** who looks after the **SHEEP**?

He's under a haystack, fast asleep.

Will you wake him? Oh no, not I,

For if I do, he'll surely **CRY** (page 82).

KEY VOCABULARY

BOY - Open and close hand at forehead

MOUSE - Brush tip of nose with index finger

UP - Move index finger upward

DOWN - Move index finger downward

GIRL - Slide thumb of closed hand from ear along jaw

SIT - Place two bent fingers on opposite two fingers

SPIDER - Stack open hands and wiggle fingers

WATER - Tap *W* hand twice on chin

Music Mayhem

You don't need fancy instruments to make music with your baby. Grab some pots and pans together with a wooden spoon, and you're ready to go! Play your favorite tunes and let baby bang along.

WHAT YOU NEED

Pots and pans
Metal and plastic bowls
Wooden spoons

Dry beans or rice
Empty water bottle

HOW-TO

Place some pots and bowls upside down on the floor. Give your baby a wooden spoon and gently tap it on the pot so they can hear the noise. Let them experiment with banging and tapping the different pots and bowls.

Ask your baby, "Do you want to listen to some **MUSIC**?" Play some music you enjoy and let baby provide the percussion.

Place some dry beans or rice in an empty water bottle (fill it about halfway). Cap the bottle and give it a little shake to demonstrate to your baby the sound your homemade maraca makes. Let your baby experiment and shake it, too!

Practice the signs for **STOP** and **GO** by prompting your baby to shake, shake, shake the homemade maraca when you say and sign **GO** and then to stop when you say and sign **STOP**.

MUSIC - Swing your dominant hand over your opposite forearm

STOP - Bring the side of dominant hand down onto opposite palm

GO - Move both index fingers away from you

Handy Tip: Music is great for your baby's brain development as well as their gross motor skills and physical coordination. Play music you enjoy in the car and around your home, and your baby will reap a lifetime of benefits.

Nice Kitty

If you have a cat or a dog, chances are your baby is pretty interested in your four-legged family member. If you don't have a pet, you probably have a friend or family member who does. If the pet is good with babies, it's a perfect opportunity to teach them the sign for **CAT** or **DOG**.

WHAT YOU NEED
A baby-friendly pet

HOW-TO
Talk to your baby about the pet. Say, "Look at the big **DOG**. He wants to smell you!" Or, "The pretty kitty **CAT** likes to have her neck scratched!"

Remind your little one that it's important to be **GENTLE** with animals. You can model the sign for **GENTLE** on your baby's hand or arm so they can feel what a gentle touch actually feels like.

KEY VOCABULARY

CAT - Pinch thumb and index finger near cheek and move outward

DOG - Pat your thigh

GENTLE - Lightly stroke the back of your opposite fist

Handy Tip: "Dog" is generally fingerspelled D-O-G in ASL. Some other variations include snapping your fingers (with or without the snapping sound) or a combination of patting your thigh and snapping your fingers. I recommend patting your thigh, which is the easiest variation for little ones.

The Wheels on the Bus

Here's a fresh take on a beloved children's song, typically done with hand gestures, like rolling your fists to show the wheels spinning. Try it using sign language to practice some of the signs you know, such as **MOM, DAD,** and even **LIGHT**!

The wheels on the **BUS** go round and round

Round and round, round and round

The wheels on the **BUS** go round and round

All through the town

The **DOORS** on the bus go open and shut

Open and shut, open and shut

The **DOORS** on the bus go open and shut

All through the town

The **LIGHTS** on the bus go blink blink blink

Blink blink blink, blink blink blink

The **LIGHTS** on the bus go blink blink blink

All through the town

The **BABIES** on the bus **CRY,** "Wah wah wah

Wah wah wah, wah wah wah."

The **BABIES** on the bus **CRY,** "Wah wah wah"

All through the town

The **MOMMIES** on the bus say, "Shhh shhh shhh

Shhh shhh shhh, shhh shhh shhh"

The **MOMMIES** on the bus say, "Shhh shhh shhh"

All through the town

The **DADDIES** on the bus say, "I love you

I love you, I love you [sign **I-L-Y**]"

The **DADDIES** on the bus say, "I love you" (sign **I-L-Y**)

All through the town

continued

KEY VOCABULARY

BUS - Line *B* hands up and slide them apart and back

DOOR - Face both palms out and pull dominant hand backward twice

LIGHT - Lift hand up and open fingers downward

BABY - Cradle your arms and rock them side to side

CRY - Slide index fingers down cheeks

MOM - Tap thumb of open hand on chin

DAD - Tap thumb of open hand on forehead

I-L-Y - Bend two middle fingers down

Handy Tip: The ASL sign for **LIGHT** depends on the type of light being described. Because the lights in this song are the headlights on the bus, hold both hands facing outward and open and close your fingers to show the bus lights flashing!

Off to the Races

Toddlers love things that go! Cars, trucks, bicycles—pretty much anything with wheels will provide tons of fun. Rolling a toy car across the floor is fun anytime, but why not make it even more fun by creating roadways and racetracks to delight and entertain your little one?

WHAT YOU NEED

Toy cars, trucks, tractors (anything with wheels)

Painter's (masking) tape or washi tape

Cardboard tubes from paper towel or gift wrap rolls

Empty tissue boxes

HOW-TO

Have your toddler help you gather some toy vehicles for the activity.

Create a roadway on your floor with masking or washi tape, both of which are easy to remove. Make the road wide enough to accommodate the largest toy vehicle your child has selected.

Make it interesting by adding curves, turns, and intersections to the road. You can make a stoplight by drawing red, yellow, and green circles on a paper towel tube and taping it in an upright position.

Make bridges and overpasses by cutting arches in an empty tissue box and taping them in place over the road.

Talk about each vehicle (**CAR, TRUCK, BICYCLE, MOTORCYCLE**) as your child plays. Say, "Oh, your **CAR** is so fast!"

Pretend to be a police officer directing traffic. Tell your little one when it's time for their **CAR** to **GO** and **STOP**.

continued

KEY VOCABULARY

CAR - Move closed fists up and down alternately

TRUCK - Move closed fists forward and backward alternately

BICYCLE - Circle your fists away from you

MOTORCYLE - Hold both fists out and twist dominant one upward twice

GO - Move both index fingers away from you

STOP - Bring the side of dominant hand down onto opposite palm

Handy Tip: If the weather's nice, you can take this activity outdoors and create roads and racetracks with sidewalk chalk. Make the roads small for little vehicles or large enough for your child to follow on a ride-on or push car.

Old MacDonald Had a Farm

Farm animals are everywhere in children's books, puzzles, clothing, and toys of all kinds. Learning the signs for common barnyard animals will create loads of signing opportunities as you play, sing, and read with your little one. Children love this song because the vowel sounds, **E-I-E-I-O** (pages x–xi), are fun and easy to say, as are the animals sounds, like "moo" and "neigh."

LYRICS

Old MacDonald had a farm
E-I-E-I-O
And on that farm he had a **COW**
E-I-E-I-O
With a "moo moo" (sign **COW**) here
And a "moo moo" (sign **COW**) there
Here a "moo," there a "moo"
Everywhere a "moo moo"
Old MacDonald had a farm
E-I-E-I-O

Old MacDonald had a farm
E-I-E-I-O
And on that farm he had a **HORSE**
E-I-E-I-O
With a "neigh neigh" (sign **HORSE**) here
And a "neigh neigh" (sign **HORSE**) there
Here a "neigh," there a "neigh"
Everywhere a "neigh neigh"
Old MacDonald had a farm
E-I-E-I-O

continued

KEY VOCABULARY

COW - Twist *Y* hand forward at temple

HORSE - Thumb at temple and twitch two fingers forward

PIG - Place hand under chin and bend all fingers downward twice

GOAT - Touch fist to chin, then *V* hand to forehead

Handy Tip: Keep repeating the lyrics using different animals for subsequent verses, like **PIG** and **GOAT**.

Peek-a-Boo Toys

Babies love peek-a-boo games. In addition to being lots of fun, peek-a-boo games help babies master the concept of object permanence—the understanding that something is still there even if it's out of sight. This skill develops during the first year.

WHAT YOU NEED

A few of your baby's favorite toys

Small blanket or towel

HOW-TO

Place a toy in front of your baby and say, "Look at the rubber **DUCK**! Quack quack [sign **DUCK**]!" Then cover the duck with a burp cloth or a small towel.

Ask your child, "**WHERE** did the **DUCK** go? Can you help me find the **DUCK** under the **BLANKET**?" See if your baby reaches for the cloth and discovers it on their own. If not,

you can pull the cloth away and say, "I found it! There's the **DUCK**!" Repeat and follow your baby's lead as you encourage them to explore and play.

You can put just about anything under the blanket, which is a great way to make introducing new sign language vocabulary more exciting.

KEY VOCABULARY

DUCK - Open and close two fingers to thumb at mouth

WHERE - Shake index finger side to side

BLANKET - Pull closed hands up chest

Five Little Ducks

Although this cute little song takes a sad turn when mama duck realizes all her little ducklings are gone, it is a playful way to introduce the sign for **SAD**. Fortunately, there is a happy ending, so you can switch from being very **SAD** to very happy as you sing and sign the last verse!

LYRICS

Five little **DUCKS** went out to **PLAY**

Over the hill and far away

MAMA DUCK said, "Quack quack quack quack" (sign **DUCK**)

But only four little **DUCKS** came back

Four little **DUCKS** went out to **PLAY**

Over the hill and far away

MAMA DUCK said, "Quack quack quack quack" (sign **DUCK**)

But only three little **DUCKS** came back

Three little **DUCKS** went out to **PLAY**

Over the hill and far away

MAMA DUCK said, "Quack quack quack quack" (sign **DUCK**)

But only two little **DUCKS** came back

Two little **DUCKS** went out to **PLAY**

Over the hill and far away

MAMA DUCK said, "Quack quack quack quack" (sign **DUCK**)

But only one little **DUCK** came back

One little **DUCK** went out to **PLAY**

Over the hill and far away

MAMA DUCK said, "Quack quack quack quack" (sign **DUCK**)

But none of the five little **DUCKS** came back

SAD MAMA DUCK went out one day

Over the hill and far away

SAD MAMA DUCK said, "Quack quack quack quack" (sign **DUCK**)

And all of the five little **DUCKS** came back

DUCK - Open and close two fingers to thumb at mouth

PLAY - Twist *Y* hands away from each other

MOM - Tap thumb of open hand on chin

SAD - Move both open hands down over your sad face

Handy Tip: Add the numbers 1 through 5 (page xii) to introduce counting to your baby and show the number of ducks decreasing through the song.

At the Playground

Head to your local playground or maybe just your own backyard! Fresh air and active play are beneficial for your baby's development, including good sleep. The sights, smells, and textures of playing outdoors provide a variety of sensory experiences to stimulate your baby. You can also meet other families and make new friends!

WHAT YOU NEED

Outdoor playground with swings and/or a slide

HOW-TO

Tell your baby you're going to go **OUTSIDE** to the playground.

Push your child in the swing. Say, "Wheeee, the **SWING** is so much fun!" Let the swing slow to a stop and ask, "Do you want me to push you **MORE** (page 25)?" Whether or not your child signs back, if they seem interested, give them another push.

Point out the sandbox or other features of the playground and ask if your toddler wants to **PLAY**.

Point out the **SLIDE** and see if your toddler is interested in climbing **UP** (page 31) and sliding **DOWN** (page 31).

If your child gets to play with another child, you can talk about their new **FRIEND** (page 26).

KEY VOCABULARY

OUTSIDE - Close fingers and move hand away from shoulder twice

SWING - Place two bent fingers on opposite two fingers and swing

PLAY - Twist Y hands away from each other

SLIDE - Slide U fingers down opposite U fingers

Row, Row, Row Your Boat

"Row, Row, Row Your Boat" is a simple song to sing with your little one. It's a great song to sing while playing with toy boats in the bathtub or with a water table. Simple songs like this are great because it's so easy to switch up the lyrics and have fun with it! Here are a few playful variations for you and your little one to enjoy.

LYRICS

Row, row, row your **BOAT**
GENTLY down the stream
Merrily, merrily, merrily, merrily
Life is but a dream!

Row, row, row your **BOAT**
GENTLY down the stream
If you see a **CROCODILE**
Don't forget to scream!

Row, row, row your **BOAT**
GENTLY to the shore
If you see a **LION** there
Don't forget to roar!

Row, row, row your **BOAT**
GENTLY down the creek
If you see a little **MOUSE** (page 72)
Don't forget to squeak!

KEY VOCABULARY

BOAT – Cupped hands move away in bouncing motion

GENTLE – Lightly stroke the back of your opposite fist

CROCODILE – Open and close your "claw" hands

LION – "Claw" hand moves from top of head down and back

This Place Is a Zoo!

Turn your home into a zoo with your child's stuffed animals! Gather up all those plush toys for some imaginative playtime and practice your animal signs and sounds. You can get creative and let your child be the zookeeper. Ask them questions about the animals, including what sounds the animals make and what they like to eat. You might get some silly answers!

WHAT YOU NEED

Stuffed animals
Laundry baskets or boxes

Blue towel or blanket

HOW-TO

Have your little one help you collect all the stuffed animals you can find and place them in a pile.

Set up laundry baskets and boxes around the room to serve as cages at your pretend zoo.

Help your child sort and group the stuffed animals into their cages to set up your zoo.

As you sort and organize the animals into their cages, show your child the sign for each. Say, "Oh, this is a big **GORILLA**! The **GORILLA** beats his chest like this."

Make a pretend watering hole for the **PENGUINS** or the **ELEPHANTS** with a blue towel or blanket.

As you talk about the animal names and signs, highlight the sounds the animals make. Say, "This is a **GIRAFFE** with a looong neck." or "This silly **MONKEY** is trying to get out of its cage! Get back in there, **MONKEY**! The **MONKEY** says, 'ooo, ooo, ahh, ahh!'"

When you're done playing, tell your little one it's time to **CLEAN** (page 28) up and put all the animals away.

TIGER - "Claw" hands move outward from face twice

BEAR - Cross arms and scratch shoulders

GIRAFFE - Extend *C* hand upward from neck

MONKEY - Scratch your sides

ELEPHANT - Fingertips swoop down and away from nose

GORILLA - Beat fists on chest

PENGUIN - Hold hands out at sides and tilt side to side

ZEBRA - "Claw" hands move back and forth across torso

CHAPTER 5

Baby's Big World

As your baby becomes a toddler, their whole world opens up to new ways of discovery. Toddlers are natural scientists, and there is just so much to explore! They want to touch, smell, hear, and, yes, taste everything they can get their hands on.

In this chapter, you'll learn signs to help expand your curious toddler's vocabulary about the world around them. You'll learn signs for colors, weather, and places in your community (like school and the library).

This chapter also includes activities to help keep your toddler both busy and safe. Teaching sign language vocabulary for movements and opposites will keep your little one moving and grooving with active games, like "Freeze Dance" and "Hop Like a Bunny." You'll also find favorites like "The Itsy Bitsy Spider" and "Mary Had a Little Lamb." In addition, songs and games with signs for feelings and keeping healthy will support your child's social and emotional development.

The Itsy Bitsy Spider

"The Itsy Bitsy Spider" is traditionally sung with hand movements, or gestures, to accompany the tune. You can replace the gestures with real ASL signs or use a combination of gestures and signs if you like. I've included two versions: one with just one sign per line and a second more advanced version. You can start with version 1 and then move to version 2 when you're more comfortable adding more signs.

LYRICS (VERSION 1)

The itsy bitsy **SPIDER**
Climbed up the **WATER** spout
Down came the **RAIN**
And washed the **SPIDER** out

Out came the **SUN**
And dried up all the **RAIN**
So the itsy bitsy **SPIDER**
Climbed up the spout **AGAIN** (page 64).

LYRICS (VERSION 2)

The itsy bitsy [sign **LITTLE**, page 40] **SPIDER**
Climbed **UP** (page 31) the **WATER** spout
DOWN (page 31) came the **RAIN**
And washed the **SPIDER** out.

Out came the **SUN**
And dried up all the **RAIN**,
So the itsy bitsy [sign **LITTLE**] **SPIDER**
Climbed **UP** the spout **AGAIN**.

KEY VOCABULARY

SPIDER - Stack open hands and wiggle fingers

WATER - Tap *W* hand twice on chin

RAIN - Move open hands downward in short motions

SUN - Draw circle with pointer, then open fingers downward

Jump! Dance! Run!

When your little one becomes more mobile, active games can help build both body confidence and coordination. This fun game allows your toddler to get their wiggles out while also teaching important self-regulation skills. Learning how to respond and react to the environment takes time, and toddlers can struggle to make transitions from one activity to the next. This game makes practicing these important skills so much fun that you'd never know you're doing important work!

HOW-TO

Stand with your toddler and ask them to copy your actions. Ask them, "Can you do what I do?"

Then say, "I'm going to **JUMP**. Can you **JUMP**, too?" Demonstrate the sign and encourage your toddler to **JUMP** along with you.

Say, "Whew, I'm so tired! I'm going to **SIT** now. Can you **SIT**?"

Then say, "Okay, I feel better now. Let's **STAND** up. Can you **STAND** up like me?"

Repeat these "monkey see, monkey do" activities while showing your little one the signs for the movements.

If your little one can sign on their own, invite them to take the lead and decide what actions you should do. Follow their instructions to **DANCE, WALK,** or **RUN**.

JUMP - Move inverted *V* hand upward from palm and bend fingers

SIT - Place two bent fingers on opposite two fingers

STAND - Place inverted *V* hand on opposite palm

DANCE - Swing inverted *V* hand over opposite palm

WALK - Lift your hands up and down like feet walking

RUN - Hook index finger on opposite thumb, bend fingers, and move away

Handy Tip: Once your child is a little older, you can use some of these signs to give more nuanced directions when needed. For example, you can sign **WALK** to prompt your child to stop running by the pool, or sign **SIT** to remind them to sit down at dinner.

Teddy Bear, Teddy Bear, Turn Around

Many children's songs and nursery rhymes incorporate movement and gestures. Using sign language builds on this same principle, allowing for clearer early communication. For songs and rhymes, you don't have to use only sign language or only gestures—you can combine them! This classic nursery rhyme provides the perfect opportunity to use both signs and movements to engage your baby in active play.

LYRICS

Teddy **BEAR**, teddy **BEAR**
Turn around (turn around)
Teddy **BEAR**, teddy **BEAR**
Touch the ground (touch ground)
Teddy **BEAR**, teddy **BEAR**
DANCE on your toes (dance)
Teddy **BEAR**, teddy **BEAR**
Touch your nose (touch nose)
Teddy **BEAR**, teddy **BEAR**
STAND on your head

Teddy **BEAR**, teddy **BEAR**
Go to **BED** (pretend to sleep)
Teddy **BEAR**, teddy **BEAR**
Say **GOOD NIGHT** (page 29)
Teddy **BEAR**, teddy **BEAR**
Turn out the **LIGHT** (page 75)
Teddy **BEAR**, teddy **BEAR**
Wake up now (pop eyes open)
Teddy **BEAR**, teddy **BEAR**
Take a bow (bow)

KEY VOCABULARY

BEAR - Cross arms and scratch shoulders

DANCE - Swing inverted *V* hand over opposite palm

STAND - Place inverted *V* hand on opposite palm

BED - Tilt head onto open hand

Nature Walk and Sorting

Head outside for a nature walk! Take your little one for a walk and explore your local area's parks and trails. Little ones love to collect the treasures they find, and this activity will turn that desire into a fun game.

WHAT YOU NEED
Basket or bag

HOW-TO

Tell your child you're going **OUTSIDE** to explore. Grab your basket or bag to collect samples from nature that you find along the way.

As you walk through your neighborhood, point out items you see, such as a **ROCK** or a **FLOWER** on the ground, showing your child the signs for those things.

As your child picks up an item, narrate their actions and invite them to start collecting what they find. Say, "You found a **LEAF**! Do you want to put it **IN** my basket?"

Continue exploring, commenting on the **GRASS, TREES,** and **CLOUDS** you see on your walk.

When you return home, sit with your child and explore the contents of your basket. Help your child sort them into groups of like items. Say, "Oh, this is a **ROCK**. Let's put this **ROCK** with the other **ROCKS** right here."

continued

KEY VOCABULARY

OUTSIDE - Close fingers and move hand away from shoulder twice

ROCK - Knock dominant fist on opposite fist

FLOWER - Touch fingers to thumb and touch both sides of nose

LEAF - Place index finger on opposite wrist and twist open hand

IN - Place fingertips inside opposite curved hand

GRASS - Brush palm of "claw" hand away from chin twice

TREE - Place elbow on opposite hand and twist your open hand

CLOUD - Swirl your "claw" hands around near your head

Handy Tip: Sorting and grouping is a developmental skill that toddlers begin to understand around age 2. If your toddler isn't interested or ready to do the sorting part of this activity, just enjoy reviewing and appreciating your collected items with your little one.

How Do You Feel?

Learning to identify emotions in oneself and in others is crucial for your child's social-emotional development. Toddlers as young as 14 months old begin to display empathy for others' feelings, showing concern when they see or hear someone crying or in distress. Giving your toddler the language to talk about their feelings is an incredible gift that they will benefit from their whole life.

WHAT YOU NEED

Pictures of people in a variety of situations with a range of emotional expressions

HOW-TO

Place your photos of people on the floor or table in front of you and your child.

See if your child touches or picks up a photo. Comment on the person in the image. Say, "That child is **CRYING**. They look very **SAD**." Or say, "That person is laughing so much! They look really **HAPPY**!"

Provide images with context to help your child understand the feelings shown. For example, for **SAD**, show a picture of a child crying with a dropped ice-cream cone on the ground.

Talk about the photos one by one. For example, say, "That child is opening his birthday present. He looks so **EXCITED**." Or "That kiddo is hiding behind their mommy's legs. I think they might be feeling **SHY**."

If you have photos of people looking **SILLY, GRUMPY,** or **SCARED**, you can use those signs, too.

continued

KEY VOCABULARY

CRY - Slide index fingers down cheeks

SAD - Move both open hands down over your sad face

HAPPY - Brush hand upward on chest

EXCITED - Bend middle fingers in and move upward alternately at chest

SHY - Twist backs of fingers outward on cheek

SILLY - Twist your Y hand in front of nose

GRUMPY - Bend fingers of "claw" hand in front of face

SCARED - Pop closed fists open in front of chest

Handy Tip: It's hard for children to learn to communicate about big feelings when they're actually experiencing those feelings. Talking about big feelings (like **SAD** or **CRY**) while doing an activity like this, or reading a book where a character is upset, provides a safe opportunity to discuss difficult emotions.

Miss Polly Had a Dolly

This cute, timeless song is a fun way to teach very useful vocabulary, like **DOCTOR, SICK,** and **MEDICINE**. Introduce these signs to your baby when they're feeling well, and you'll be able to use them when they get sick and need to visit the doctor. It's even more fun for baby if you use a playfully serious voice when the doctor says, "Miss Polly, put her straight to **BED**!"

LYRICS

Miss Polly had a **DOLLY** who was **SICK, SICK, SICK**

So she called for the **DOCTOR** to come quick, quick, quick

The **DOCTOR** came with his bag and his **HAT** (page 46)

And he knocked on the **DOOR** (page 82) with a rat-a-tat-tat

He looked at the **DOLLY** and he shook his head

He said, "Miss Polly, put her straight to **BED**!" (page 50)

He wrote out a paper for a pill, pill, pill (sign **MEDICINE**)

"I'll be back in the **MORNING** (page 29) with my bill, bill, bill."

KEY VOCABULARY

DOLL - Slide bent index finger down nose twice

SICK - Tap bent middle finger to forehead and abdomen

DOCTOR - Tap three fingers on inside of opposite wrist

MEDICINE - Touch bent middle finger to opposite palm and lightly shake

---

Handy Tip: If you're not familiar with this song's tune, search for videos of it online and you'll find lots of good examples.

Pretend Library

Take a trip to the library without actually leaving the house! With just a few props and the books you already have, you can set up a pretend library at home for some fun playtime with your little one. Toddlers love this game because it lets them put the books in the book return, which at the real library is often too high to reach.

WHAT YOU NEED

Large cushions or pillows
Cardboard box

Assortment of children's books
Backpack

HOW-TO

Set up a cozy reading nook with some cushions or throw pillows in a corner.

Create a book drop by turning an empty cardboard box upside down and cutting a slot in the bottom big enough for a book.

Set books out for display on shelves or low tables.

Give your child an empty kid-size backpack or bag and tell them you're going to play **LIBRARY**.

Say to your child, "Let's go to the **LIBRARY** and get some **BOOKS**! You can put the **BOOKS IN** your **BACKPACK** and then we'll go **READ** together."

Let your child fill their bag with books and then head to the reading nook you set up to read the books.

When you're done with reading time, tell your child, "It's time to go back to the **LIBRARY** and take the **BOOKS** back. We're **ALL DONE** with these **BOOKS**."

Show your child how to "return" the books by dropping one in the book-return box. Then ask, "Do you want to put the **BOOKS IN** the box?"

LIBRARY - Circle your *L* hand at your shoulder

BOOK - Place flat hands together and open outward

BACKPACK - Tap your *C* hands at your shoulders

READ - Move inverted *V* hand over opposite palm

ALL DONE - Twist open hands away from you

IN - Place finger-tips inside opposite curved hand

Feel the Weather

Learning about the weather engages your child's senses. But you don't have to wait for snow or rain to teach your child the signs for **COLD, HOT,** and **WIND**. Learn some easy hacks for introducing weather-related vocabulary to your child—no storm required!

WHAT YOU NEED

Frozen vegetables or chilled teether

Plastic colander

Food processor

Bowl and spoon

Sock and dry rice

Hair dryer or fan

HOW-TO

Let your baby touch a bag of cold vegetables or a chilled teether and talk about how **COLD** it is.

Stand with your baby in front of the refrigerator and say, "Brrrrr! It's so **COLD** in there!"

At bath time, give your child a plastic colander. Fill it with water and hold it up so your baby can see the water dripping out. Say, "Look, it's **RAINING** in our bathroom!"

Place ice in the food processor to make some homemade **SNOW**. Place the "snow" in a bowl with a spoon or measuring cup and let your toddler scoop and play with it.

Fill a sock with some dry rice and tie the end tightly. Microwave for just a few seconds, and shake to make sure it's not too hot. Let baby touch the warm sock and talk about how **HOT** it feels.

Stand with your baby in front of a fan and say, "The fan is making it so **WINDY** in here!" You can also use a hair dryer on the cool setting from a safe distance to create the sensation of **WIND**.

COLD - Hold fists at shoulders and shiver

RAIN - Move open hands downward in short motions

SNOW - Move open hands downward while wiggling fingers

HOT - Place "claw" hand at mouth and twist away quickly

WIND - While palms face each other, sweep hands side to side

Handy Tip: Always use common sense and caution when playing with items that have been chilled or warmed. Test the temperature of items before letting baby touch them.

Manners Song

Young children don't really begin to understand the meaning of courtesies like "please" and "thank you" until they are three or older, but that doesn't mean you can't introduce the concept and start practicing during the toddler stage. This simple song provides some signs that will come in handy as your toddler moves into the preschool years.

LYRICS (SUNG TO THE TUNE OF "FRÈRE JACQUES")

PLEASE and **THANK YOU**

PLEASE and **THANK YOU**

I'm **SORRY**, I'm **SORRY**

Let's be **FRIENDS** (page 26) and **SHARE**

Let's be **FRIENDS** and **SHARE**

Magic words, magic words

KEY VOCABULARY

PLEASE - Circle flat hand on chest

THANK YOU - Move flat hand away from chin

SORRY - Circle closed fist on chest

SHARE - Swing dominant hand over the top of opposite hand

Handy Tip: The best way to teach your child to have good manners is to model good manners yourself. When your little one shares a bite of their food with you, say and sign **THANK YOU**. Or ask your partner to **PLEASE** pass the salt. In time, your child will follow your example.

Freeze Dance

It's time for a freeze dance! The rules of a freeze dance are simple: Dance to the music and freeze when the music stops. You can do this activity to any type of music your family enjoys—kids' music, pop, country, R&B, you name it! The most important rule is to have fun and enjoy moving your body to the beat.

WHAT YOU NEED
Music that makes you want to dance!

HOW-TO

Tell your little one you're going to do a freeze dance and they'll have to **STOP** when the music stops.

Play some music that you and your child enjoy. Start dancing and say, "I love this **MUSIC**. It makes me want to **DANCE**! Can you **DANCE** with me?"

Turn the music off suddenly and tell your child, "The music **STOPPED**, so we **STOP**."

Stand very still. If your child moves, encourage them to wait for the music to start by signing and saying **WAIT**. Say, "**WAIT** for the **MUSIC** to start."

Start the music again and say, "Okay, now we **DANCE**!"

Don't be afraid to be silly and make up some crazy dance moves. Your child will love seeing your goofy side.

continued

KEY VOCABULARY

STOP - Bring the side of dominant hand down onto opposite palm

MUSIC - Swing your dominant hand over your opposite forearm

DANCE - Swing inverted *V* hand over opposite palm

WAIT - Wiggle fingers of both hands in front of you

Handy Tip: This game is more fun with friends! If you have neighbors or family visiting, this is a great way to get the kids moving and to burn off some energy. Older kids usually know this game well, so toddlers can follow their example.

Colors of the Rainbow

Babies begin to recognize colors by around 18 months, but it can take a few years to really master learning and naming colors. Here are some fun ways to introduce colors to your little one in an age-appropriate way. Just remember that your child will learn to identify and label colors in their own time, so just have fun with it!

WHAT YOU NEED

Bathtub finger paints
Colored construction paper
Masking tape

Colored pom-poms
Craft paper
Washable markers

HOW-TO

Identify and label colors in your everyday conversations with your child. Say, "Let's put your shirt on. This shirt is **ORANGE**."

Give your toddler choices when possible. Ask them, "Would you like your drink in the **BLUE** cup or the **RED** cup?"

Bring bathtub finger paints into the tub at bath time and let your toddler "paint" in the tub. Talk about the colors they're using. Say, "Oh, you put lots of **GREEN** on the wall. **GREEN** is a pretty **COLOR**."

Tape some construction paper to the floor with masking tape. Make a small pile of colored pom-poms on the floor in colors that match the construction paper colors. Help your child place pom-poms on the paper that matches. Say, "Let's put this **YELLOW** pom-pom on the **YELLOW** paper."

Give your child a plain sheet of craft paper and some washable markers. Let them create their own masterpiece. Narrate their artistic process and label the colors as they draw. Say, "You're making some beautiful art with the **RED** marker." Or comment, "Look at all the **PURPLE** color on the page!"

continued

KEY VOCABULARY

ORANGE - Squeeze fist open and closed under chin

BLUE - Shake your *B* hand

RED - Slide index finger from mouth down chin

GREEN - Shake your *G* hand

COLORS - Wiggle fingers on chin

YELLOW - Shake your *Y* hand

PURPLE - Shake your *P* hand

What's the Weather?

This simple song is an easy way to practice your weather-related signs as part of your daily routine. Look out the window with your toddler to see what it looks like outside. Ask them, "What do you see **OUTSIDE** (page 90)? I see **SNOW**. It's a **SNOWY** day. We should put on our **COAT** (page 46) before we go outside!"

LYRICS (SUNG TO THE TUNE OF "TWINKLE, TWINKLE, LITTLE STAR")

Look **OUTSIDE** now; can you see
WHAT (page 22) the weather's going to be?

Is there sunshine (sign **SUN**)? Is there **RAIN** (page 95)?
Is the **WIND** blowing hard again?

Are there snowflakes (sign **SNOW**) falling down?
Are there big **CLOUDS** floating 'round?

Look **OUTSIDE** now; can you see
WHAT the weather's going to be?

KEY VOCABULARY

SUN - Draw circle with pointer then open fingers downward

WIND - While palms face each other, sweep hands side to side

SNOW - Move open hands downward while wiggling fingers

CLOUD - Swirl your "claw" hands around near your head

Handy Tip: Discussing the temperature and weather with your child before leaving the house might reduce struggles about what to wear.

Muddy Trucks

Messy play is so fun and exciting for little ones. But you might worry about the mess or your child putting yucky things in their mouth. If you're up for a bit of messy play, your toddler will love the sensory experience of playing with trucks in edible "dirt" or "mud." If the weather's nice, you can do this activity outside. I liked to let my kids do messy activities like this in the bathtub when they were little—makes for easier cleanup!

WHAT YOU NEED

Graham crackers
3 cups flour (optional)
1 cup cocoa powder (optional)

2 cups brown sugar (optional)
Plastic bin or foil roasting pan
Toy trucks and tractors

HOW-TO

Make edible dirt or sand by grinding up graham crackers in a food processor or blender.

For messier play, make edible mud by combining flour, cocoa powder, and brown sugar together. Add water to the consistency you'd like.

Place the dirt or mud in a plastic bin or foil pan, and add trucks and tractors.

Invite your child to drive and dig in the dirt with their trucks and tractors. Comment about how **DIRTY** the vehicles are getting. Say, "The **TRUCKS** are so busy digging in the dirt. It's so fun to **PLAY** and get messy (sign **DIRTY**)!"

When it's time to wrap up, let your child know: "It's time to **CLEAN** up! Let's get you and the **TRUCKS** all **CLEAN**."

DIRTY - Place hand under chin and wiggle fingers

TRUCK - Move closed fists forward and backward alternately

PLAY - Twist *Y* hands away from each other

CLEAN - Slide flat hand along opposite palm

Handy Tip: The sign for **TRACTOR** is the same for **TRUCK**. It's like a bigger version of the sign for **CAR**.

Potty Song

Potty training is a huge milestone for toddlers, and communication is key because many toddlers are still building their vocabularies. Signing can help your child let you know when they need to go, and this song will help both of you learn and master these useful signs. This is sung to the tune of "Apples and Bananas" but "I'm a" replaces "I like to" and "big kid now" replaces "eat eat eat."

LYRICS

I'm a big kid now
I pee (sign **POTTY**) on the **POTTY**
I'm a big kid now
I **POOP** on the **POTTY**

I'm a big kid now
I can use the **POTTY**
I'm a big kid now
I can use the **POTTY**

Oh, I wash my hands (sign **WASH HANDS**)
After I go **POTTY**
Oh, I wash my hands (sign **WASH HANDS**)
After I go **POTTY**

KEY VOCABULARY

POTTY - Shake your *T* hand

POOP - Grab thumb of dominant hand and pull down

WASH HANDS - Rub your hands together

Obstacle Opposites

When your child is young, you don't need a big climbing structure to provide opportunities for gross motor play. You can create a fantastic obstacle course using items around the house. Homemade obstacle courses provide a perfect way to practice vocabulary and signs for opposites, like **UP, DOWN, IN, OUT, STOP,** and **GO**.

WHAT YOU NEED

Couch cushions and throw pillows
Laundry basket
Balls or beanbags

Blanket
Chairs

HOW-TO

Create an obstacle course in your home by creating a variety of physical activities and challenges for your toddler. Use signs for opposites as your child moves through the tasks.

Pile couch cushions for your child to climb. Say, "You climbed **UP** on the pillows. Can you climb **DOWN** to the floor now?"

Set up a laundry basket with balls or beanbags to toss into the basket. Invite your child to throw the balls **IN** the basket. Once all the balls are in the basket, ask your child to take them **OUT** and do it again.

Create a tunnel for your toddler to crawl through by draping a blanket over chairs. Invite them to go **IN** the tunnel, and wait for them on the other end. As they're crawling through, say, "You're **IN** the tunnel! Come on **OUT**."

You can make the obstacle course a race by having your child do the activities in a sequence. Use the timer on your phone to see how long it takes to do them all. Tell your child to **GO** when you start the timer, and sign **STOP** when they finish the course. Or just cheer them on to go faster, faster!

continued

KEY VOCABULARY

UP - Move index finger upward

DOWN - Move index finger downward

IN - Place finger-tips inside opposite curved hand

OUT - Pull finger-tips out of opposite curved hand

GO - Move both index fingers away from you

STOP - Bring the side of dominant hand down onto opposite palm

Mary Had a Little Lamb

This is a classic nursery rhyme, but we often hear just the first verse. The second and third verses make the song a lot more fun and silly!

LYRICS

Mary had a **LITTLE LAMB**
LITTLE LAMB, LITTLE LAMB
Mary had a **LITTLE LAMB**
Its fleece was white as **SNOW** (page 107).
And everywhere that Mary went
Mary went, Mary went
And everywhere that Mary went
The **LAMB** was sure to **GO** (page 79).

He followed her to **SCHOOL** one day
SCHOOL one day, **SCHOOL** one day
He followed her to **SCHOOL** one day
Which was against the rules.

It made the children **LAUGH** and **PLAY** (page 44)
LAUGH and **PLAY**, **LAUGH** and **PLAY**
It made the children **LAUGH** and **PLAY**
To see a **LAMB** at **SCHOOL**.

KEY VOCABULARY

LITTLE - Move open hands toward each other

SHEEP - Move fingers like scissors up opposite arm

SCHOOL - Clap your dominant hand down on opposite palm twice

LAUGH - Move index fingers out from corners of mouth twice

Handy Tip: In ASL, "lamb" combines the signs for **BABY** (page 19) and **SHEEP**. To avoid confusion, sign **LITTLE** and **SHEEP** instead.

Oh, No! Baby's Sick!

A pretend medical kit is a great toy for a toddler, but if you don't have one, you can improvise with household items. Pretending to be the doctor caring for a "sick" baby doll is a great way to prepare your child for an upcoming checkup with your pediatrician and help them learn signs related to health and wellness.

WHAT YOU NEED

Low table or a bin

Toy medical kit or medical supplies, like bandages, bulb syringe, and thermometer

Baby dolls and/or stuffed animals

Washable markers

HOW-TO

Set up a pretend doctor's office using a low table or upside-down bin as an exam table. Gather your toy medical kit or other medical supplies. If using real supplies, be sure to supervise your child closely with things like bandages and thermometers.

Have your child help you gather some dolls and/or stuffed animals and seat them near your exam area. Explain how the **DOLLS** are your patients and that they are all **SICK** or **HURT** and need to see the **DOCTOR**.

Bring the first patient to the **DOCTOR** and have your child assess what's wrong with them. Are they **SICK**? Do they need some **MEDICINE**? Maybe they fell down and their leg is **BROKEN**.

If you have a plastic doll, you can create "boo-boos" by drawing on the doll with a washable marker. A little wipe with rubbing alcohol will take it right off when it's "healed."

Have fun pretending to care for your patients to help them feel better!

DOLL - Slide bent index finger down nose twice

SICK - Tap bent middle finger to forehead and abdomen

HURT - Point index fingers at each other

DOCTOR - Tap three fingers on inside of opposite wrist

MEDICINE - Touch bent middle finger to opposite palm and lightly shake

BROKEN - Hold fists out and move both downward sharply

If You're Happy and You Know It

Singing about a variety of feelings in this classic children's song is a great way to practice feelings signs so that your toddler can use them when needed. When using signs for emotions, it's important that your facial expressions match the meanings of the signs, and you can take that even further by exaggerating your expressions and really hamming it up!

LYRICS

If you're **HAPPY** and you know it, then you **LAUGH** (say, "Ha ha!")

If you're **HAPPY** and you know it, then you **LAUGH** (say, "Ha ha!")

If you're **HAPPY** and you know it and you really want to show it

If you're **HAPPY** and you know it, then you **LAUGH** (say, "Ha ha!")

If you're **SAD** and you know it, then you **CRY** (say, "Boo hoo!")

If you're **SAD** and you know it, then you **CRY** (say, "Boo hoo!")

If you're **SAD** and you know it and you really want to show it

If you're **SAD** and you know it, then you **CRY** (say, "Boo hoo!")

If you're **GRUMPY** and you know it, stomp your feet (stomp feet and say, "Stomp stomp!")

If you're **GRUMPY** and you know it, stomp your feet (stomp feet and say, "Stomp stomp!")

If you're **GRUMPY** and you know it and you really want to show it

If you're **GRUMPY** and you know it, stomp your feet (stomp feet and say, "Stomp stomp!")

If you're **EXCITED** and you know it, shout hooray (say, "Hooray!")

If you're **EXCITED** and you know it, shout hooray (say, "Hooray!")

If you're **EXCITED** and you know it and you really want to show it

If you're **EXCITED** and you know it, shout hooray (say, "Hooray!")

HAPPY - Brush hand upward on chest

LAUGH - Move index fingers out from corners of mouth twice

SAD - Move both open hands down over your sad face

CRY - Slide index fingers down cheeks

GRUMPY - Bend fingers of "claw" hand in front of face

EXCITED - Bend middle fingers in and move hands upward alternately at chest

Little Schoolhouse

Let's play school! Playing school, especially being the teacher, was my younger kiddo's favorite activity as an older toddler and preschooler. It's just so much fun to be in charge when you're little! You can create your own little schoolhouse at your kitchen table or coffee table. Playing school is also a great time to learn the signs for useful things, like **TEACHER, BACKPACK**, and more.

WHAT YOU NEED

Table and chair

Stuffed animals

Books

Paper

Markers

Scissors

Backpack

HOW-TO

Set up a table and chair to be the teacher's desk. Chances are your child will want to be the teacher! Say, "Let's play **SCHOOL**! Do you want to be the **TEACHER**?"

You can play the student, or you and your child can set up their stuffed animals to be the students.

Invite your child to "art class." Get some paper and pencils. Say, "Let's **WRITE** and **DRAW** (page 126) together. We can use these **PENCILS**!"

It's circle time! Help your child set their stuffed animals in a half circle to listen to a **BOOK** (page 65). Allow your little one to pick a **BOOK** to **READ** to the students. You can help read the book while your child turns the pages.

It's time to go **HOME**. Encourage your child to pack their **BOOKS** in their **BACKPACK** because **SCHOOL** is **ALL DONE** (page 25) for today.

SCHOOL - Clap your dominant hand down on opposite palm twice

TEACHER - Closed fingertips move away from temples, then flat hands move downward

CLASS - Move *C* hands in a circle away from you

READ - Move inverted *V* hand over opposite palm

WRITE - Move pinched fingers across opposite palm

PENCIL - Touch pinched fingers to lips and move across opposite palm

HOME - Touch closed fingers near mouth and then to cheek

BACKPACK - Tap your *C* hands at your shoulders

Handy Tip: The signs for **ART** and **DRAW** (page 126) are the same in ASL.

I Love You Hands

Create a sweet keepsake of this special time in your little one's life by making paper "I love you" hands. This simple craft will freeze time for a moment so you can remember just how small your child's hand was compared with your own.

WHAT YOU NEED

Pencil
Plain paper
Scissors

Glue stick
Construction paper

HOW-TO

Trace your hand on a piece of paper while narrating for your baby: "I'm going to **DRAW** my hand with a **PENCIL** (page 125) on a piece of **PAPER** and cut it out with **SCISSORS**."

Trace your child's hand on another piece of paper and cut it out.

Gently bend the middle two fingers down on each hand and glue the bent fingertips

to the palm of each hand so it looks like the sign for "I love you" (sign **I-L-Y**).

Arrange and glue the two hands on a piece of construction paper in the color of your choice.

Make sure to document the date and your child's age on your creation!

KEY VOCABULARY

I-L-Y - Bend two middle fingers down

DRAW - Move pinky in swirling motion across opposite palm

PAPER - Brush palms together in opposite directions

SCISSORS - Open and close two fingers like scissors

Hop Like a Bunny

Hop like a bunny! Slither like a snake! Challenge your toddler to move their body like a variety of animals, like a **PENGUIN,** a **FISH,** and even a **TIGER**! This active game will get the wiggles out while also letting you and your little one practice some animal and movement signs.

HOW-TO

Ask your child, "Can you hop [sign **JUMP**] like a **BUNNY** (page 72)?"

Show your toddler the sign for **TIGER** (page 93). Growl like a tiger as you say, "This is the sign for **TIGER**. The **TIGER RUNS** very fast. Can you **RUN** like a **TIGER**?"

Pretend you're a **FISH** (page 62) swimming. Sign **SWIM** as you swim around the room.

The sign for **PENGUIN** (page 93) involves moving in a waddling motion like a penguin's **WALK**. Teach your child the sign for **PENGUIN** and walk like penguins around the house.

KEY VOCABULARY

JUMP - Move inverted *V* hand upward from palm and bend fingers

RUN - Hook index finger on opposite thumb, bend fingers, and move away

SWIM - Face palms outward and move in swimming motion

WALK - Lift your hands up and down like feet walking

Resources

AUTHOR'S WEBSITE

Visit me online for virtual classes as well as many helpful articles: TinySigns.com.

ONLINE VIDEO DICTIONARY

You might find it helpful to see the signs you've learned in this book in action. I've created a free video dictionary of all the signs in this book on my Tiny Signs website, where you can find short videos of me demonstrating each of the signs as well as all the signs from my other books. Access the video dictionary at TinySigns.com/book-owner.

BOOKS

Baby Sign Language Made Easy: 101 Signs to Start Communicating with Your Child Now **by Lane Rebelo**

The perfect book for beginners! You'll find easy instructions on my top 101 American Sign Language signs for babies, directions on how to get started, and answers to all your questions.

The Complete Guide to Baby Sign Language: 200+ Signs for You and Baby to Learn Together **by Lane Rebelo**

Ready to learn more? Expand your signing vocabulary with the popular follow-up to *Baby Sign Language Made Easy* for more signs, tips, and activities.

My First Book of Baby Signs: 40 Essential Signs to Learn and Practice **by Lane Rebelo**

Part storybook and part sign language guide, this adorable book is designed to encourage you and your baby to learn new words and signs as you read together.

ASL RESOURCES

If you'd like to learn more about American Sign Language and the Deaf community, the following sites are a great place to get started. You can also search online for any in-person ASL classes that might be offered in your area.

Gallaudet.edu/asl-connect

Gallaudet University in Washington, D.C., is the only university in the world where students live and learn using ASL and English. They offer a variety of both free and paid online ASL courses that are open to all.

Lifeprint.com

Run by Dr. Bill Vicars, an ASL professor in California, Lifeprint.com has a ton of useful information about ASL. Dr. Vicars also has a fantastic YouTube account.

SignItASL.com

This site features online classes led by a variety of talented and knowledgeable Deaf instructors. These classes use a lot of humor and storytelling to make learning fun!

Index

ACKNOWLEDGMENTS

Thank you to my mom for instilling in me a love of music. The classic children's songs in this book were learned by your side at the piano, the place of my favorite childhood memories.

Thank you to Callisto Media and my editor, Mo Mozuch, for yet another opportunity to share my love of baby sign language with the world.

Thank you to Andre, Clara, and AJ for making sure I had time to write. You're my three favorite people in the whole world.

And most of all, thank you to the Club Tiny Signs community. I love learning and signing with you!

ABOUT THE AUTHOR

 **Lane Rebelo, LCSW**, is the author of the best-selling *Baby Sign Language Made Easy*, *The Complete Guide to Baby Sign Language*, and *My First Book of Baby Signs*. She's a mother of two and the founder of Tiny Signs®, an award-winning baby sign language program. As a licensed social worker, Lane worked for many years with families in the Boston area. Lane began studying American Sign Language in 2006 after her first baby was born and was amazed by all she had to say. She lives with her husband and two children in MetroWest Boston. Find her online at TinySigns.com.

Printed in the USA
CPSIA information can be obtained
at www.ICGtesting.com
JSHW040500210524
61733JS00009BA/19